Revelation

Revelation is a bewildering text, rich in imagery and full of extraordinary symbols and events. It claims to tell the story of 'what must soon take place' and yet, despite centuries of scholarly research, the order and content of this story has remained one of the greatest mysteries of all time.

Alan Garrow's perception of the text as designed for serial presentation provides a basis for a new and orderly understanding of the structure of the story. This development makes possible a new and coherent interpretation of 'what must soon take place'.

According to this study, John discerned a close relationship between the present and the End. For today's readers, as for the members of the seven churches, this insight has profound implications for the way in which world events, weekly worship and everyday choices are perceived.

A.J.P. Garrow is an Anglican priest in Waltham Abbey, Essex.

New Testament Readings
Edited by John Court
University of Kent at Canterbury

EPHESIANS
Martin Kitchen

JOHN'S GOSPEL
Mark W.G. Stibbe

2 THESSALONIANS
Maarten J.J. Menken

MARK'S GOSPEL
John Painter

Forthcoming books in this series:

GALATIANS
Philip Esler

ACTS
Loveday Alexander

JAMES
Richard Bauckham

Revelation

A.J.P. Garrow

London and New York

First published 1997
by Routledge
11 New Fetter Lane, London EC4P 4EE

Simultaneously published in the USA and Canada
by Routledge
29 West 35th Street, New York, NY 10001

Typeset in Baskerville by 10/12 pt. at
Pure Tech India Limited, Pondicherry
Printed and bound in Great Britain by
Redwood Books, Trowbridge, Wiltshire

British Library Cataloguing in Publication Data
A catalogue record for this book is available from the British Library

Library of Congress Cataloging in Publication Data
Garrow, A.J.P. (Alan John Philip), 1967–
Revelation/A.J.P. Garrow.
    p. cm. – (New Testament readings)
    Includes bibliographical references and index.
    1. Bible. N.T. Revelation–Commentaries. I. Series.
    BS2825.3.G37   1997   96–26318
    228'.07–dc20   CIP

ISBN 0–415–14640–2 (hbk)
      0–415–14641–0 (pbk)

To John and Kate

Contents

Series editor's preface

This volume has every right to stand on its own, as a significant contribution to the study of the book of the New Testament with which it is concerned. But equally it is a volume in a series entitled *New Testament Readings*. Each volume in this series deals with an individual book among the early Christian writings within, or close to the borders of, the New Testament. The series is not another set of traditional commentaries, but is designed as a group of individual interpretations or 'readings' of the texts, offering fresh and stimulating methods of approach. While the contributors may be provocative in their choice of a certain perspective, they also seek to do justice to a range of modern methods and provide a context for the study of each particular text.

The collective object of the series is to share with the widest readership the extensive range of recent approaches to Scripture. There is no doubt that literary methods have presented what amounts to a 'new look' to the Bible in recent years. But we should not neglect to ask some historical questions or apply suitable methods of criticism from the Social Sciences. The origins of this series are in a practical research programme at the University of Kent, with an inclusive concern about ways of using the Bible. It is to be hoped that our series will offer fresh insights to all who, for any reason, study or use these books of the early Christians.

John M. Court
Series Editor

Author's preface

To the well-worn saying, 'A journey of a thousand miles begins with a single step,' I would like to add, 'but it helps if you set off in the right direction'. The same may be said of the study of Revelation.

One of the first steps in the interpretation of any extended text is the apprehension of that text's structure. The fact that there is no generally recognized understanding of the structure of Revelation provides an important clue as to why, despite many hundreds of years of scholarly analysis, a convincing interpretation of Revelation has proved so elusive.

The central objective of this reading, therefore, is to address the problem of the structure of Revelation. This is the subject of the extended Chapter 3, in which is presented the theory that Revelation was designed to be read aloud in six separate instalments. The chapter makes progress where other scholarly analyses (reviewed in Chapter 2) have faltered, in that a chronologically consistent set of story-telling passages are disclosed.

This structure makes possible the reconstruction of two important aspects of the text's original context: that created by the text itself, and that created by the theatre of its reception. In combination with a renewed understanding of the date and historical context of Revelation (Chapter 4) it has been possible to apply the technique of audience context reconstruction (outlined in Chapter 1) to the analysis of John's story. The result, in Chapter 5, is a new and coherent interpretation of 'what must soon take place'.

The interpretation of this story itself raises further questions, in that John's future prediction did not come about on the time-scale that he proposed. The reason for this is considered in Chapter 6, where Revelation is presented as a polemic response to the competing future predictions, and attendant calls for allegiance, of John's day.

If the interpretation of Revelation may be likened to a journey of a thousand miles, then this reading is little more than a single step. However, I hope that it is one which will set off the interested novice, as well as the expert scholar, in a direction which will result in a fruitful engagement with John's masterpiece.

I must allow some particular individuals to represent the five groups of people that have made possible the completion of this book. The first is Dr Peter Cotterell of the London Bible College. It was he who first introduced me to the potential power of discourse analysis in the interpretation of texts. The second is Dr R.T. France of Wycliffe Hall, Oxford. His was the spark of enthusiasm which gave me the courage to begin the research of which this book is a product, and his encouragement throughout the last five years has greatly assisted in its completion. The third is Professor Lars Hartman of the University of Uppsala. Conversations with Professor Hartman, during a period of study financed by the Cleaver Ordination Candidates Fund, provided good-humoured guidance amid the potential minefield of text-linguistic analysis. The fourth is Canon Patrick Hobson of Waltham Abbey Church, Essex. His patience, and that of many friends and colleagues, has made the completion of this project possible, as has the typing of Barbara Jacobs. Final thanks are reserved for my family, who have borne with me for many years, even the ones during which I have been caught up in Revelation.

Alan Garrow
Waltham Abbey
February 1996

Acknowledgement

Scripture quotations are from the New Revised Standard Version of the Bible, copyright 1989 by the Division of Christian Education of the National Council of the Churches of Christ in the USA. Used by permission. All rights reserved.

Chapter 1

An introduction to this reading of Revelation

If you have ever had to listen to someone who speaks incredibly quickly and equally unintelligibly, then you may have pondered this question: 'Is my inability to understand this person due to my lack of intelligence, or is it because they are talking complete nonsense?' Reading Revelation can provoke a similar response. In snatches and passages the text displays an authority and lucidity that makes the reader eager to understand more. At other times it seems to disintegrate into a cacophony of disordered images that appear to defy reason and obscure understanding. The aim of the following reading is to disentangle this confusion and so make it possible to hear with greater clarity what the whole text meant to its original intended audience, and so what it might have to say to us today.

A clarification of the aim

Any examination of a text that claims to deal with the question of that text's 'meaning', must explain in some detail what kind of meaning is being referred to: the author's intended meaning or the receiver's perceived meaning. Knowledge of the author's intended meaning would be of supreme value in the case of Revelation because this would allow the interpreter to understand precisely what the author 'John' (whose precise identity will be considered on pp. 53–9) had to say to his audience about the nature of the universe and its future destiny. With the benefit of this knowledge it would also be possible to offer an authoritative evaluation of other interpretations of the text, some of which have been used for the unscrupulous manipulation of the beliefs and wallets of others. However, despite the importance of the author's intended meaning, it is *always* inaccessible to anyone reading any text, apart from the author him or herself. This is simply because anyone (who is not the author) who reads a text to perceive its meaning, must, by definition, be creating a receiver's perceived meaning.

Given that the author's intended meaning is inaccessible, it is necessary to concentrate on the idea of the receiver's perceived meaning. In contrast to the author's intended meaning the receiver's perceived meaning is not unique, since there can be as many receiver's perceived meanings as there are receivers. This is possible because of the way in which the perceived meaning of a particular word or group of words is dependent on its context. Context is defined here as the receiver's total experience of the world prior to interpreting a particular word or group of words. The previous experience of a receiver determines the significance attributed to a word, or group of words, because the interpretation of any communication is dependent on previous experience of similar words in similar contexts (Cotterell and Turner 1989: 41). Because the experience of every person is unique every individual will interpret each text in a unique way. To some extent this is the case but this does not mean, as may be inferred, that it is therefore impossible for an author to communicate a particular message with 'good enough' accuracy. This is because authors are not helpless; if they know the context in which text will be received, then they can take account of this so that the words in the text are those which, in the context of the receivers, are those which are most likely to be perceived as the author intends. Revelation was written for a particular group of audiences whose contexts were known to the author: the congregations of the seven churches of Asia Minor. It may therefore be expected that John wrote his text so that his words would have been received in contexts that would be most likely to lead his audience towards the perception of his intended meaning.

In summary, the author's intended meaning is the goal towards which this reading aspires. However, because this meaning is not accessible it is necessary to attempt to establish, as far as possible, the original intended receiver's perceived meaning, since this is the meaning that is likely to approximate most closely to the author's intended meaning.

THE METHOD

So far it has been suggested that the meaning of a text is dependent on the context in which it is read, and that the context of the original intended receivers is that which will reveal the closest approximation to the author's intended meaning. Therefore, the method of approach employed in this reading will be to reproduce the context of the original intended receivers as closely as possible.

One aspect of the receiver's context which it is possible to ascertain with a high degree of accuracy (perfect accuracy would require access to the autograph manuscript, and fortunately there are remarkably few textual variants in Revelation) is the context created by as much of the text as has already been received (hereafter referred to as the 'co-text'). This aspect of context can have a profound effect on the receiver's perceived meaning, as demonstrated by this example from Brown and Yule (1983: 139, 140):

1   *A Prisoner Plans His Escape*
Rocky slowly got up from the mat, planning his escape. He hesitated a moment and thought. Things were not going well. What bothered him most was being held, especially since the charge against him had been weak. He considered his present situation. The lock that held him was strong, but he thought he could break it.

2   *A Wrestler in a Tight Corner*
Rocky slowly got up from the mat, planning his escape. He hesitated a moment and thought. Things were not going well. What bothered him most was being held, especially since the charge against him had been weak. He considered his present situation. The lock that held him was strong, but he thought he could break it.

The fact that (1) and (2) are commonly read as communicating distinctly different meanings suggests that the co-textual context created by the different headings influences the interpretation of the subsequent text. Hence, this reading will seek to pay close attention to how the author uses the text itself to create particular contexts which guide the receivers' interpretation of subsequent portions of text.

(Because the interpretation of a particular group of words may be influenced by text which follows that passage, as well as text which precedes it, it should be noted that the co-textual context includes all the text on either side of a particular word or group of words.)

A second aspect of context is the 'theatre of reception'. The exact environment in which a text is going to be received is not known by most authors. For example, I don't know whether you are reading this in a library, in your home, surrounded by people, on your own. Because you could be in any situation I cannot allow the intelligibility of my text to be dependent on a particular 'theatre of reception'. In contrast it appears that John did expect his text to be received in a particular setting. Revelation 1.3 indicates that he expected it to be read aloud (Bauckham 1993a: 3; A. Y. Collins 1984: 144; Barr 1986: 243). Revelation 1.11 and 2.1–3.22 suggest that it was designed to be read to congregations. If the text were read at a Sunday service then it may have been accompanied by a Eucharist (cf. Acts 20. 7–11), a possibility made more likely by the number of eucharistic references in the text (Barr 1986: 253–5). The specificity of this theatre means that the following reading will consider the possible influence of this aspect of context on the original intended receivers' perceived meaning.

A third aspect of context is the historical context. This includes all the receivers' experience of the world before encountering the text, e.g. their knowledge of the political history of the region, contemporary and ancient literature, social circumstances, religious practices, etc. Changes in the receiver's experience of these factors can produce a great variety of different perceived meanings (as illustrated by the range of interpretations of Revelation proposed by non-intended readers through the centuries). An accurate assessment of the receivers' historical context is therefore of very considerable importance in the interpretative process. In order to reconstruct a picture of the hearers' historical context, so far as this is possible, it is necessary to establish the date of Revelation (cf. Chapter 4).

There is little new in a method of approach which gives attention to the original context of the text. However, traditional analyses of the context of Revelation have tended to focus on the text's historical context (e.g. Caird 1984: 3–7), while failing to pay sufficient attention to those aspects of context over which John had specific control or particular knowledge: the co-textual context and the context created by the theatre of reception. By studying these neglected aspects of context, in combination with the wider historical context, it should be possible to reproduce with a new degree of accuracy the context in which John's hearers received Revelation. The consequence of this will be an improved understanding of how John's intended hearers interpreted his text.

Chapter 2

The problem: where and what is the story?

In Revelation 1.1 it is claimed that the text will reveal to its intended hearers, 'what must soon take place'. This title provides a co-textual context for the whole of the rest of the text and is therefore of supreme importance (Brown and Yule 1983: 139–40; Traugott and Pratt 1980: 404). That this is the essential cause of confusion is expressed by Sweet:

> The purpose of the revelation is to show his servants what must soon take place.... But the scenes and events which John goes on to describe are repetitive and jump back and forth in time; as they stand they cannot be made to fit a linear time-scale.
>
> (Sweet 1990: 58)

Fiorenza has sought to deny that the promise of a chronological story exists (1985: 46, cf. p.10), but its presence is stubbornly re-stated at three other significant points: in Revelation 1.10b–20 John is commissioned by Christ to prophesy to the churches and the content of this prophecy is stated in 1.19 as: 'what is and what is to take place after this'. In 4.1 the voice from heaven provides a co-textual context for the main vision cycle by saying: 'Come up here, and I will show you what must take place after this.' The main vision cycle closes at 22.5 and in 22.6 the angel reflects on the vision saying: 'These words are trustworthy and true, for the Lord, the God of the spirits of the prophets, has sent his angel to show his servants what must soon take place.' This confirms in retrospect that the story of what must soon take place, which was promised at the start, has indeed been told.

These important indicators of the presence of a story are supported by evidence of the author's desire to influence his hearers' behaviour in the light of his prediction of future events. For example, in the seven messages there is consistent association between approved behaviour and final reward (2.7, 11, 17, 26–28; 3.5, 10–12, 21) and between disapproved behaviour and final punishment (2.4–5, 14–16, 20–23; 3.2–3, 15–19). (In the rest of the text there are similar clear references to the consequences of actions (e.g. 7.14–17; 14.4–5; 16.5–6; 20.4–6; 21.7–8)). If the behaviour of the intended hearers were to be modified on this basis, then the proposed future consequences of approved and disapproved behaviour would have to be both intelligible and convincing to them.

Evidence from the title and behavioural goal of the text combine to suggest that the story of 'what must soon take place' would have been intelligible to John's intended hearers. The fact that this information has been hidden from non-intended readers is the central problem for any student who wants to uncover the intended hearers' perceived meaning. The initial challenge for those who are non-intended readers of Revelation is, therefore, to locate the story or explain why it is absent. This process begins with an assessment of scholarly progress in this area.

A REVIEW OF SCHOLARLY APPROACHES TO THE STORY IN REVELATION

While there are many different scholarly approaches to Revelation, two points are held in common by the vast majority of them. First, that the text tells a story and that characters within the text ought to experience the main story events in the following order: (a) persecution of Christians; (b) punishment of persecutors; (c) salvation of the persecuted (A. Y. Collins 1984: 112); or some such similarly logical scheme (cf. Farrer 1964: 7, 23; Bauckham 1993a: 266–318; Fiorenza 1985: 47). Second, that these story events are not presented in a straightforward sequence. Charles is sometimes cited as contradicting this consensus (Mounce 1977: 45), but this is not the case. Charles states, '[Revelation] exhibits, except in short passages...a structural unity and a steady development of thought from the beginning to 20.3. In 20.4–22, on the other hand, the traditional order of the text exhibits a hopeless mental confusion and a tissue of irreconcilable contradictions' (Charles 1920: I, VI, 1).

Despite these areas of broad agreement there is a profound lack of consensus as to why the story of 'what must soon take place' is not straightforwardly discernible to non-intended readers. The range of proposed reasons for the obscurity of the story-line may be grouped under five headings.

The story has become incoherent in the process of composition

Some scholars have suggested that Revelation lacks consecutive development in its story-line because it has been constructed from various earlier apocalypses (Charles, Gaechter, Boismard, Rousseau and Ford as reviewed in Fiorenza 1985: 161 and Mazzaferri 1989: 8–32). However, the weight of evidence in support of the compositional unity of Revelation means that this position is not accepted by the majority of scholars (e.g. Swete, Bousset, Zahn, Beckwith as reviewed in Fiorenza 1985: 161). Bauckham goes so far as to say, 'The more Revelation is studied in detail, the more clear it becomes that it is not simply a literary unity, but actually one of the most unified works in the New Testament' (1993a: 1). A more sophisticated version of the compositional theory is that an original text was revised or altered in some way (cf. Fiorenza 1985: 162 for review). However, for such revisions to have destroyed the coherence of the book it is necessary to posit an incompetent editor (as Charles does (1920: I, IV, 1)), or some such, as the perpetrator of violence to the original, presumably coherent, text. A third view is that Revelation was composed from a collection of fragments of various oral and written traditions (cf. Fiorenza 1985: 162 for review). There is certainly evidence for a variety of sources (as there is in any extended text), but for the author to be so ruled by these traditions as to produce an incoherent text himself requires incompetence or an, as yet, unconsidered explanation.

Whether taken individually or in combination all these theories present the final author/redactor as incapable of preserving coherence in the text. This is not an impossible interpretation, but it is one which should be treated with circumspection given the evidence of compositional care provided by the text's unity of language and by certain elements of its structural development.

The story is incoherent because of the genre of the text

Kiddle (1940: xxvii–xxxiii) describes the book as a poem that follows no logical plan but builds up the impression of inevitable judgment. This view imposes a simple genre on the text without recognizing the self-statements of the text on this matter. Indications within the text of its literary type are by no means transparent, but the fact that it nowhere describes itself as a poem weakens Kiddle's case.

Sweet sees Revelation as a report of an ecstatic vision. According to him this factor means that: 'we must reckon with an element of incoherence and with the building up of impressions after the manner of music rather than logical argument' (1990: 43–4). This is not an impossible solution but it is weak in two respects. First, there is the evidence of careful composition; second, the self-description of the text as apocalyptic narrative (1.1), prophecy (1.1, 3), and epistle (1.4). All these, and every other generic indicator in the text, suggest the author's intention to communicate coherently with his audience.

An alternative to seeing the incoherence of the story as a product of the text's genre, is to see incoherence as a product of our inability to identify the correct genre. It is widely recognized that genre identification is vital to the interpretative process (Cotterell and Turner 1989: 97–100). A good deal of work has been undertaken in this field with a particular focus on the question of defining the genre 'apocalypse' or the genre of Revelation (J.J. Collins 1979; Aune 1986; Hellholm 1986). This process has been useful insofar as the genre 'apocalypse' has been identified as a sub-genre of narrative; however, it has already been noted that this is an insufficiently sophisticated conclusion to account for the complex organization of the story in Revelation. It is therefore necessary to go on to consider how the interrelation of multiple generic characteristics may have contributed to complex story organization in Revelation. Some work has been done on Revelation as liturgy, drama or myth (cf. Fiorenza 1985: 164–70 for review), but none of these approaches has so far provided a convincing account of the organization of the story in Revelation.

The story is obscured by its complex structural arrangement

Scholars who see Revelation as a crafted unity suggest various structural arrangements of the text which are said to reveal the correct organization of story elements. All of these theories make use of the idea that the same basic story is retold, or 'recapitulated', at different points throughout the text. Victorinus presented this type of structural theory in the third century (quoted in Lambrecht 1980: 80). More recent supporters have been Beasley-Murray (1978: 30–2), A.Y. Collins (1984: 111–16), Lambrecht (1980: 77–104), Bornkamm (1937: 132–49 – quoted in Lambrecht) and Sweet (1990: 44). Various versions have been suggested.

In its least elaborate form the recapitulation theory focuses on the series of judgments which accompany the breaking of the seals, the blowing of the trumpets and the emptying of the bowls. Beasley-Murray presents his conclusion thus:

> Are chapters 6–19 to be viewed as continuous narration of events leading to the parousia? Or are we to regard the three series of messianic judgments, set forth under the symbolism of the seals, trumpets, and cups of wrath, as parallel? The present writer is persuaded that the latter interpretation alone accords with the evidence.
>
> (Beasley-Murray 1978: 30)

Lambrecht (1980: 103) provides an extensive exploration of the slightly more complex theory that, 'The author of Revelation combines recapitulation and progression.' Sweet (1990: 44) and Court (1994: 85) also subscribe to this type of theory. Caird (1984: 104–6) sees the seven series as progressive recapitulations of the whole story, adding the idea that the unnumbered visions provide detailed attention to parts of the story.

The weakness of the case for a recapitulation theory, as it applies to the three series of sevens, is inadvertently made clear by Lambrecht's own tabular presentation of the 'most striking' parallelisms (1980: 88–90; see also Rowland's similar table, 1993: 82). This table shows the distinct lack of comparison between the seal visions and the trumpet and bowl visions. (A link between the trumpet and bowl visions *is* made clear by this table, the reason for which will be considered on p.23)

A. Y. Collins takes the recapitulation theory a step further by suggesting that:

> The book of Revelation is composed of two great cycles of visions, 1.9–11.19 and 12.1–22.5. Each of these cycles is made up of three series of seven: (1) seven each of messages, seals, and trumpets; (2) (seven) unnumbered visions, (seven) bowls, and another series of (seven) unnumbered visions. . . . Beginning with the seven seals, each series expresses the whole message of the book in its own particular way. The constant elements of the message are (a) persecution, (b) punishment of persecutors and (c) salvation of persecuted.
>
> (A. Y. Collins 1984: 111–12)

Collins' solution does contain genuine insights: she is willing to include the whole text, not just the series of sevens, and there is an important recognition of a former 'veiled cycle' and latter 'revealing cycle'. However, there are crucial weaknesses in her theory. First, her appeal to unnumbered visions; if the author had intended such a numbering, then it is curious that these numbers were not supplied as they are in the other series (Lambrecht 1980: 83). Further, as Bauckham observes (1993a: 17), Collins' numbering of the second series of 'unnumbered visions' is contrived in that there are more than seven visions which fulfil her criteria for this type of vision. Second, Collins' claim that each section expresses the whole message of the book 'in its own particular way' does not satisfactorily explain why the story elements in each of her proposed series still appear in an eccentric order. For example, in the first series (6.1–8.5), the order of 'message elements' is: punishment (6.1–8), persecution (6.9–11), punishment (6.12–17) and salvation (7.1–17). In the second series the order is: punishment (8.1–10.11), persecution (11.1–11), salvation (11.11–12) punishment (11.13–14), review of all three (11.15–18). These categorizations are not Collins', nor are they particularly refined, but they serve to indicate that Collins' structuration has the effect of creating small conundrums rather than solving the problem of the specific story told by the whole text. Similar repetitions and sequential disorganization of story elements may be found in each of Collins' proposed series, with the exception of the fourth series.

The text is thematically and not temporally organized

Fiorenza states, 'previous attempts to explain the sequence of visions or the total composition of Revelation either by a linear or cyclic understanding of time have not succeeded in presenting a convincing interpretation' (1985: 46). This assessment leads Fiorenza to conclude that Revelation is not structured according to a 'temporal–historical' sequence, but consists of eschatological themes which are ordered in a concentric pattern (1985: 46). This structure, taken from Fiorenza 1991: 35–6, is an annotated version of the structure described in Fiorenza 1985: 175.

A 1.1–1.8 Prologue and Epistolary Greeting
B 1.9–3.22 Rhetorical Situation in the Cities of Asia Minor
C 4.1–9.21; 11.15–19 Opening the Sealed Scroll: Exodus Plagues
D 10.1–15.4 The Bitter Sweet Scroll: 'War' against the Community
C' 15.1, 5–19.10 Exodus from the Oppression of Babylon/Rome
B' 19.11–22.9 Liberation from Evil and God's World-City
A' 22.10–22.21 Epilogue and Epistolary Frame.

A close examination of Fiorenza's position exposes an important weakness: the apparent belief that conventional time-lines become unnecessary in matters concerning eschatology. That this is Fiorenza's position is suggested by her statement that 'the main concern of Revelation is not [salvation] history, but eschatology' (1985: 46). An appeal to the eschatological priority of Revelation is used by Fiorenza as a means of avoiding questions of chronology, and yet the above quotation goes on to define eschatology as: 'the breaking-in of God's kingdom and the destruction of the hostile godless powers'. This in itself implies an order of events (the present order followed by the breaking in of a new order). Fiorenza concedes as she continues:

> The author of Revelation is, indeed, aware of time, but he knows only a 'short time' before the eschaton. The eschatology of Revelation is, therefore, not dependent on or legitimated by a certain course of historical events. Rather, time and history have significance only insofar as they constitute the 'little while' before the end.
>
> (Fiorenza 1985: 46)

This focus on the 'little while' may be justified, but it does not discharge the text of its responsibility to provide a chronologically intelligible account of the contents of the 'little while'. The describing of the course of the history from the hearers' present until the End is central to a vital function of apocalyptic literature; that is, the explanation of how present events are in continuity with God's overall plan, despite apparent evidence to the contrary.

In actuality Fiorenza does talk in temporal terms in much of her discussion of the eschatological expectation of Revelation. The elements of story that she mentions are essentially the same as Collins': persecution followed by punishment of persecutors followed by salvation of the persecuted. The following quotations illustrate this type of temporal progression within Fiorenza's thematic framework. 'The author does not ask about the meaning of history and its temporal sequence, but rather about the meaning of the present situation of the community and the date of God's judgment on those dwelling on earth' (1985: 47). 'The description of God's judgment takes up such a large space in Revelation that its whole eschatological presentation culminates in judgment and salvation' (1985: 47). 'The goal and high point of the composition of the whole book, as of the individual "little apocalypses," is the final judgment and the eschatological salvation' (1985: 47). This is, however, a progress of types of event; Fiorenza studiously denies that Revelation is concerned with describing the detail of how one event proceeds from another. Given that a convincing account of how the progression of story elements will be worked out in the experience of the hearer is necessary for the purpose of the text, Fiorenza's denial of a consecutive story-line is the principal weakness of her position. Without this denial the concentric arrangement of story elements has a strong contribution to make to the story-line debate. The case for a different concentric presentation of the story will be made on pp.15–35.

The story is told and then expanded

Bauckham identifies the story as that which is contained within the sealed scroll of Revelation 5.1, which he also sees (following Mazzaferri) as identical to the 'little' scroll of 10.2. By identifying the little scroll with the sealed scroll Bauckham is able to suggest that the story which the sealed scroll contains is divulged after the open 'little' scroll has been ingested by the prophet (10.10). Bauckham sees the content of the scroll as described in a nutshell in 11.1–13, and then expanded in the remaining chapters of Revelation (1993a: 266).

This approach emphasizes the important point that the story of 'what must soon take place' is contained within the scroll of Revelation 5.1. This is a reasonable conclusion given the promises to reveal the story of 'what must soon take place' in Revelation 1.1 and 4.1; where 1.1 creates the expectation that the whole text will somehow reveal this story, and 4.1 focuses this expectation on the immediately ensuing text by saying: 'Come up here, and I will show you what must take place after this.' Despite this the next two chapters provide no new story information, instead they present the scroll of 5.1 as the ultimate container of revelatory information. In 5.5 this scroll is described as the exclusive revelatory preserve of the Lamb (cf. 1.1), which is given to him by God himself in 5.7 (cf. 1.1). All eyes and voices are then focused on these two central characters, and the scroll, as the four living creatures, the elders, myriads of myriads and thousands of thousands of angels (5.11) and every creature in heaven and on earth and under the earth and in the sea (5.13) bow down to worship before the scroll is opened. These events mean that there can be little doubt about the importance of the scroll, and, in the light of 4.1, it may be concluded that it contains the revelation of 'what must soon take place'. In order to perceive that story, therefore, it is only necessary to identify the contents of the scroll. Having recognized this important step towards locating the story, Bauckham (1993a: 249) continues: 'Commentators are at a loss to identify the contents [of the scroll] convincingly.' Even this assessment is charitable, since it is more often the case that scholars have assumed that the contents of the scroll start to be revealed as the seals are broken (or in some cases when the trumpets are blown) and that this revelation continues uninterrupted until 22.5 when the main vision cycle closes. Rather than being 'at a loss', therefore, most scholars have been oblivious to the fact that their identifications of the contents of the scroll are problematic and unconvincing.

Asking the right question is half the battle, and to this extent Mazzaferri and Bauckham have made a vital contribution to the search for the story. As the only scholars to give detailed consideration to this question their arguments will be considered in detail in Chapter 3, in which the search for the story will be continued.

SUMMARY

There are several points of insight amongst the scholarly positions considered above which are worth noting before continuing the search for the story. These include: the unity of the text; the importance of genre for interpretation and the possible influence of genre on the structural scheme of the text; persecution, punishment and salvation as basic elements of the story; the presence of duplications of these story elements; the possibility of a concentric pattern in these duplications; the identification of the sealed scroll as the container of the story of what must soon take place.

However, the problem remains that, while most scholars recognize that the purpose of Revelation is to reveal to John's audience what must soon take place, this story remains elusive. This puzzle is explained, by the majority of scholars (with the exception of Mazzaferri and Bauckham), in one of two ways. Either, the editor was incompetent and the story was lost in the process of composition, or, the author deliberately created a text where the story is extremely difficult to follow. The crafted unity of the text makes the former option highly unlikely. The latter would be considerably more convincing if scholars were able to agree on how this story is supposed to be arranged. This lack of consensus is in fact a sign of hope, since it suggests the possibility that it is our incompetence, rather than that of the author, which is causing the problem. Careful listening to the co-textual context, and consideration of the influence on the structure of the text exerted by the theatre of reception, may yet reveal a convincing understanding of the whereabouts and logic of the story.

Chapter 3

Finding the story in the text

In its title Revelation promises to reveal to its hearers the story of what must soon take place (1.1). In 5.1–9 a heavenly scroll is presented as the container of that information (Bauckham 1993a: 263). And yet, from 6.1 onwards, the story that is promised appears to dissolve into chaos.

This situation is not unlike that of someone who buys a flat-pack bedside cabinet from a furniture store and takes it home in great excitement, only to find that the assembly instructions are missing. The hapless assembler knows that the various pieces must fit together so as to create a useful unit, but which bit does what, and what bit fits where? Without the instructions various random attempts at assembly result in frustration. Ultimately it is concluded that this is not a bedside cabinet at all, but an abstract piece of sculpti-furniture which expresses its form in terms of furniture-like themes and elements, while remaining intentionally non-functional.

Fortunately, this scenario is only apparently similar to the predicament of scholars attempting to understand story organization (structure) in Revelation. A foundational hypothesis of this reading is that the 'instructions for assembly' have been included with the text, but that they need to be listened to with closer attention than they have been in the past. Until now most exegetes have assumed that the whole text has a roughly uniform function with respect to the telling of the story. In contrast, I believe that there are a variety of different functions performed by different sections of text which, in combination, work together to tell the story of what must soon take place in an engaging and convincing way. These different functions will now be identified by considering co-textual indicators and the influence of the theatre of reception on the structure of the text. When this process has been completed it will be possible to locate those sections of text which reveal the story contained within the scroll, at the same time as establishing the different relationships which other parts of the text have to these passages.

FORESHADOWING TEXT

The purpose of this section is to assess the function of the following passages: the seal visions (6.1–17), the vision of the fate of the faithful (7.9–17), the trumpet visions (8.2–9.21), the thunders incident (10.3–4) and the contents of the little scroll (11.1–13). More specifically, the aim of this section is to assess the functional relationship of the above-mentioned passages to those parts of Revelation which directly reveal the content of the main scroll, where the term 'direct' is used to describe visions which may be crudely seen as readable straight from the scroll.

The relationship of these passages to the content of the scroll has been considered by some scholars. Despite differences between the detail of their conclusions all of these scholars imply that at least one of the above-mentioned passages represents a direct revelation of events which are described in the main scroll, and that later direct revelations of the scroll's contents re-describe the same events, albeit from a different point of view (e.g. Beasley-Murray 1978: 31; A.Y. Collins 1984: 112; Bauckham 1993a: 284, 449.) In contrast to this view I will seek to demonstrate that none of these passages directly reveal the contents of the scroll. Instead, it will be argued that all these passages foreshadow those contents.

In order to understand what is meant by 'foreshadow' in this context it is necessary to note the relationship between foreshadows and suspense.

Suspense is defined as partial uncertainty about 'what will happen'. For example in *Julius Caesar* the dictator is warned to: 'Beware the Ides of March'. This warning creates certainty that disaster awaits the emperor on 15 March, but there is suspense in the uncertainty as to exactly what will happen.

This suspense is created by a foreshadow. A foreshadow is defined as an announcement of a future occurrence in the story-line which leaves the audience partially uncertain as to the exact nature or timing of that event. In the example above this function is performed by the warning to beware 15 March (cf. Chatham 1978: 48, 59–60).

When applying this terminology to Revelation, and the question of whether or not certain passages directly reveal the contents of the scroll or merely foreshadow them, then the meaning of foreshadow may be expressed more specifically as follows: a foreshadow of the contents of the scroll is an announcement of those contents which preserves partial uncertainty about their exact nature.

Having made this excursus into definitions it is now possible to consider the functional options for the passages in question.

The first thing to note about this group of passages is that they come immediately after an important point of suspense with respect to the main scroll. By the end of Chapter 5 the hearers are certain that the scroll contains vital information about what will happen *to them* soon, but they are uncertain as to exactly 'what will happen'. In these circumstances three options are available to the author. Either, he may resolve that partial uncertainty by directly revealing the contents of the scroll, or, he may ignore the question of the contents of the scroll, or, he may maintain that partial uncertainty, while continuing to address the question of the contents of the scroll, by foreshadowing the scroll's contents.

The fact that the scroll appears centre-stage in the unsealing process which begins at 6.1 suggests that the option to ignore the subject of the scroll has not been taken. If the option to resolve suspense by directly revealing the contents of the scroll is taken at any point in the block 6.1–11.13, then it should be clear to the hearers that the contents of the scroll are being revealed directly. In these circumstances a coherent story of what must soon take place should also be apparent, since that is what the hearers were waiting for.

If the author chose to maintain suspense by foreshadowing the contents of the scroll, then it should be clear that the visions in these passages cannot be 'read' direct from the scroll. Further, these visions should be in the form of announcements which preserve partial uncertainty in the mind of the hearers as to exactly what the scroll contains.

The question of whether John chose to sustain or resolve suspense with regard to the exact contents of the scroll will now be considered in relation to each of the aforementioned passages.

The six seal visions: 6.1–17

The first question which must be asked when seeking to establish whether or not these visions represent the direct revelation of the contents of the scroll is whether or not the contents of the scroll may be revealed before all the seals have been broken.

Bauckham (1993a: 249–50) observes that, 'Most [commentators] think that the contents are progressively revealed as the Lamb opens the seven seals (6.1–8.1). But it would be a very odd scroll to which this could happen. Normally all the seals would have to be broken before the scroll could be opened.' Bauckham goes on to refute the arguments of Ford (1975: 92–3), regarding the character of ancient documents. A.Y. Collins (1976: 22), discusses the lack of evidence for the form of scroll, favoured by Roller and Bornkamm, which has a sealed part and an open readable part. Mazzaferri (1989: 271) concludes that there is: 'One [scroll] totally sealed by each of the seven external, visible seals'. Mounce (1977: 151) and Ladd (1972: 81) support this view, seeing 6.1–7.17 as an overture to the reading of the scroll in 8.2ff.

Lambrecht (1980: 81) refutes this assessment, claiming that it is not the reading of the scroll but the breaking of the seals that begins God's punitive action. However, when God's punitive action begins is not at issue, since the author would have seen evidence of this action throughout the ages, including his own. The question is rather, when does the revelation of the contents of the scroll of *final* judgment begin? The answer to which is, when the scroll has been opened – which requires the removal of all the seals which seal it shut.

The passage which immediately follows 6.1–17 also supports the suggestion that the scroll cannot be opened until all the seals have been removed. If the contents of the scroll (which include the acts of final judgment) were already spilling out, then it would not be possible for the angels of 7.1 to hold back the winds of judgment. Further, the fact that the faithful are given a protective seal at this point suggests that that which they are being protected against (the final judgment), has not yet begun. If this were not the case the act of sealing would be analogous to shutting the stable door after the apocalyptic horse has bolted. Beasley-Murray (1978: 142) and Wilcock (1975: 79) argue against this point by suggesting that the four winds are alternative symbols for the four riders on the grounds that Zechariah 6.5 refers to his four charioteers as winds or spirits. If this were the case then the restraint of the four winds must have taken place before the winds/riders were sent forth in Chapter 6. However, the identification of the riders with the winds is unlikely, since the riders are commissioned to go out from the focus of heaven (the throne) to the corners of the earth. The winds, on the other hand, will come in from the corners of the earth to its centre.

In summary, it has been argued that the content of the scroll cannot be revealed until all the seals have been broken for two reasons. First, it is not possible to open a scroll without removing its seals. Second, for an exception to this rule to be made here would create confusion in an otherwise entirely feasible event sequence.

The fact that the seal visions cannot be read direct from the scroll means that it is possible to say that John did not choose to resolve suspense with regard to the contents of the scroll. However, in order to demonstrate that these visions foreshadow the scroll's contents it is necessary to show that they announce those contents in a way that sustains suspense (partial uncertainty).

The four horsemen are classic foreshadowing images. These characters are messengers sent out to warn the four corners of the earth about the disasters which will pour forth from the scroll when it is eventually opened.

That the horsemen are messengers is indicated by the fact that each horseman rides alone (with the exception of the fourth who is accompanied by Death and Hades). This is significant inasmuch as single horsemen in military situations are very commonly messengers or envoys, for example: Esther 8.10, 14; 2 Kings 9.18; Zechariah 1.8–11 and 6.1–8. (There is no biblical example of a horseman sent by a superior, who is not a messenger or envoy.) That they ride singly is evident from three factors. First, there is no mention of a following army. Second, there is the close parallel with Zechariah's horsemen and chariots (Zechariah 1.8–11; 6.1–8), which are sent separately to the four points of the compass. Third, each rider is called out in turn by the four living creatures which stand, 'around the throne, on each side of the throne' (4.6). Having been called from four different sources it is natural to suggest that the riders would be likely to continue to travel, in the imagination of the hearers, in four different directions.

That the four riders are sent out to warn the four corners of the earth is strongly suggested by the above evidence that they travel alone. A further indication of this function may be given by 6.8 in which the fourth rider is given 'authority over a fourth of the earth'. Commentators commonly assume that this image implies that the riders destroy a fourth of the earth (Caird 1984: 81, 104; Farrer 1964: 125; Sweet 1990: 178). However, it is also possible that the use of 'a fourth' refers to commission to the riders to warn one quadrant of the earth each, so that the whole earth has an opportunity to repent before the final judgments contained in the scroll are executed.

Rather than delivering their warning message verbally the riders communicate what is to come by means of their actions. In order to understand how this is possible it is necessary to note John's view of history as repeating itself in intensifying cycles until the End. Expressions of this philosophy of history may be found elsewhere in the New Testament. For example, the Lord's Supper is seen as an event which will be repeated and intensified in the messianic banquet (Matthew 26.29; 1 Corinthians 11.26). Also in Mark 13, wars, earthquakes and famines are described as the beginning of labour pangs. This image implies repeated cycles of suffering, gathering in intensity, until the End. When history is seen in this way it is possible to point to events in the past as foreshadowings of events in the future. This appears to be the case with the rider visions in that the disasters which the riders bring are likely to have had echoes in the real past experience of John's hearers (cf. Caird 1984: 79–81). It is therefore possible that John intended to use the riders as a means of suggesting to his hearers that past disasters were sent by God to warn of the imminence and nature of the final judgments contained in the scroll.

The fifth vision foreshadows the contents of the scroll by means of an overheard conversation in which the martyrs are told that their number will be increased and then vindicated (6.11). In overhearing this conversation John's hearers would have been able to predict that the contents of the scroll would include descriptions of further martyrdoms followed by ultimate vindication.

The sixth vision is different from the other five. The hearers are not informed of what the scroll will contain by being invited to interpret the significance of events in the world or by being enabled to 'listen in' on information given to characters within the text. However, the precedent set by the first five seal visions creates the expectation that the sixth seal vision will have a similar function with respect to the scroll. The finality of the image which it portrays means that if it were not a foreshadowing, then the hearers could be forgiven for believing that the story was over before it had begun. However, when taken as a foreshadowing this vision does not create chronological confusion. Instead it has the effect of raising expectations as to the magnitude of what the scroll will be shown to contain when its contents are finally released.

If the theory that the seal visions foreshadow the contents of the scroll is correct, then we may expect to see the events which these visions foreshadow revealed in full when the contents of the scroll are finally divulged (cf. pp.61–2). This expectation is fulfilled as follows.

Vision one describes the conquering activity of a Parthian warrior. That the first rider is a Parthian is made almost certain by his representation as a mounted archer, a combination known only in the regions of the east beyond the Euphrates (Magie 1950: 402–3; Court 1979: 61; Sweet 1990: 159). As such the first rider foreshadows the events described in Revelation 16.12: 'The sixth angel poured his bowl on the great river Euphrates, and its water dried up, to prepare the way of the kings from the east.' Revelation 17.12 and 17.17 interpret this event as the destruction of Rome by Nero *redivivus* and his Parthian allies (cf. pp.95–9).

The next three visions foreshadow three aspects of judgment prior to the End. Vision two speaks of civil war, thus foreshadowing the events described in Chapter 17 in which Nero *redivivus* destroys the city which he once ruled (17.16, 17). Vision three speaks of famine, thus foreshadowing the effects of the judgments enacted in 16.2–12 and the consequences of civil war. Vision four speaks of war, famine, pestilence and wild beasts, the first three of which suggest the judgments of 16.2–12, and the consequences of civil war. The fourth may be an allusion to the role of wild beasts in the execution of Christians which might be expected to follow Nero's return to power. That these foreshadowings are not exact and not in strict order does not negate their function, since foreshadowings are designed to create or maintain suspense by preserving partial uncertainty about exactly what will happen, and when.

Vision five warns of further martyrdoms. These are described in 13.7, 15. This vision also assures the hearers that vengeance will be exacted when the white-robed army of martyrs has reached its complete number. This element of the story is described in 19.11–21.8.

As Bauckham (1993a: 208) notes, vision six bears a particular resemblance to 20.11–15. '[Both] are explicitly passages in which the earthquake accompanies the theophany of God as Judge. Moreover in these two cases John employs the tradition of the cosmic quake, in which the heavens as well as the earth flee from God's presence'. He continues: 'The vision of the sixth seal may then be intended already to point forward as far as the Last Judgement' (1993: 209). There may also be an allusion to the earthquake of Revelation 16.18–21.

To summarize: the form and content of each of the seal visions points towards the contents of the scroll and gives some indication of what those contents will be while preserving partial uncertainty (suspense) as to exactly what those contents will prove to be. These visions should therefore be taken as foreshadowings of the contents of the scroll, rather than direct revelations of those contents.

The vision of the fate of the faithful: 7.9–17

The primary function of Revelation 7.9–17 is to combine with Revelation 7.1–8 in declaring the spiritual security of God's faithful people throughout the final judgments. Further reference to how this function is fulfilled is given on pp.60. However, the overall function of 7.9–17 is considered here because, it will be argued, the method by which the overall function of 7.1–17 is achieved includes the use of a foreshadowing account of the ultimate fate of the faithful in 7.9–17.

The spiritual security of God's faithful people throughout the coming judgments is indicated by two visions of the faithful: one before the judgments and one after. As Sweet (1990: 147) puts it: 'the scene [7.1–8] is not part of the sixth unsealing; it relates to the present time, while 7.9–17 belongs to the Age to Come'.

That 7.3–8 represents the 'before' picture is apparent for three reasons: first, this sealing occurs at a high point of tension with respect to the opening of the seals (only one seal still holds the scroll shut). At this point the hearers would need reassurance that they will be protected from the ensuing judgments. This reassurance is given by showing that they will be marked with God's seal of ownership before they face persecution and possible martyrdom (Sweet 1990: 146, 147 and Bauckham 1993a: 216). Second, the description of the 144,000 shows that they are an *earthly* community, since they are protected from disasters which will affect the earth (e.g. 7.3). Third, John hears their number, but sees the multitude. Some scholars have noted a parallel between the way in which John *hears* a report about the Lion of Judah (5.5), but actually *sees* the Lamb (5.6) (Caird 1984: 96; Sweet 1990: 125–6, 150–1; Bauckham 1993a: 216). This may suggest that the past images that John hears find their eschatological fulfilment as that which John sees. The fact that John hears the community of the faithful may therefore imply that they are a pre-eschaton community.

That 7.9–17 represents an 'after' picture is apparent from its juxtaposition with the previous vision; here John *sees* the arrival of the 144,000 at their final destination.

The content of the vision also clearly identifies it as foreshadowing the final state of the faithful. They wear the white robes of those who have passed through the tribulation (7.14; cf. 6.11); they dwell in the presence of the Lamb (7.9); and join the throng and the bliss of heaven (7.9–17). As Caird (1984: 102) says, this passage is, 'in almost every detail an anticipation of the joys of the celestial city' (notably 7.15–17 parallels 21.3b–4).

In summary: none of Revelation 7.1–17 can represent the direct revelation of the contents of the scroll because the scroll is still held shut by one seal. The overall function of this passage is to give assurance of the spiritual security of God's people by presenting two pictures of them, one before the contents of the scroll have been revealed and one after. Evidence which suggests that 7.9–17 has the function of displaying the 'after' picture, and hence foreshadowing events contingent upon the opening of the scroll, includes John's visual apprehension of the multitude in 7.9–17, the blissful state in which they appear and the full description of this bliss towards the end of the text (21.1–8).

The six trumpet visions: 8.2–9.21; 11.14

The following discussion of the trumpet visions will concentrate on 8.2–9.21. However, it should be recognized that the sixth trumpet vision does not close until 11.14 when it is stated: 'the second woe [sixth trumpet] has passed. The third woe [seventh trumpet] is coming very soon.' For this reason the argument that the trumpet visions foreshadow the contents of the scroll should be seen as extending to include 10.1–11.13. However, the function of this latter section will be dealt with separately below.

The first step in the consideration of the function of the trumpet visions is to consider the functional options. These are, as it turns out, identical to those encountered at 6.1. This is because, while the hearers are still anxious to discover the contents of the scroll, these contents have only been foreshadowed by the seal visions and so full, direct revelation is still awaited. The natural tendency of the hearers would have been to assume that suspense resolution (the direct revelation of the contents of the scroll) would follow the breaking of the seventh seal (8.1). (This assumption is made by Mounce 1977: 178 and Bornkamm 1937 quoted in Lambrecht 1980: 81.) Therefore, if the option of suspense maintenance is taken by the author this must be clearly and immediately indicated.

The arrival of trumpets in 8.2 settles the question. The appearance of trumpets is a suitable indicator of suspense maintenance because of the long association of trumpets with announcements. Trumpets are used in the Bible to announce liturgical events (e.g. Leviticus 25.9), battles (e.g. Judges 3.27; 6.34; 1 Samuel 13.3; Nehemiah 4.20), eschatological disaster (e.g. Isaiah 27.13; 51.27; Ezekiel 33.2–6; Joel 2.1; Zechariah 9.14) and eschatological gathering (e.g. Matthew 24.31; 1

Thessalonians 4.16). A specific parallel may be seen in the trumpets which precede the fall of Jericho in Joshua 6. Bauckham (1993a: 205) suggests that: 'If (John) had an Old Testament precedent it could only have been Jericho.' Similarly Caird (1984: 108) says: '(John) must have had this story (the fall of Jericho) in mind when he wrote (the trumpet series).' Parallels between these two incidents include: the presence of seven trumpeters (Joshua 6.4; Revelation 8.2); six preliminary blasts (Joshua 6.3–11; Revelation 8.6–9.21); a final blast which commands action (Joshua 6.20; cf. Revelation 10.7); the presence of the ark (Joshua 6.7; Revelation 11.19), and the fall of the city (Joshua 6.20; Revelation 11.13). The degree of similarity between the two stories leads towards the conclusion that, just as the preliminary trumpet blasts announced the end for Jericho, so the blasts which precede the seventh trumpet in Revelation announce the end for the city of God's opponents. As Sweet (1990: 159) says: 'The trumpets which follow the half-hour of prayer do not give the contents of the scroll.... They are warning blasts, summoning the world to repentance.'

A supplementary indicator of the announcing function of the trumpet visions is the undisputed correlation between the final three trumpets and the three woes, to the extent that these trumpets are the three woes (8.13; 9.12; 11.14). In all thirty-three occurrences of 'woe' in the New Testament, outside Revelation, the term is used to warn of future doom (cf. also Revelation 12.12); hence, the trumpet visions should also be taken as having this type of announcing function.

These announcements preserve partial uncertainty about the actual contents of the scroll (in other words they maintain suspense by foreshadowing those contents) by refusing to describe a full and final version of events. There are two dimensions of partiality in the visions. First, only part (one third) of the various arenas is affected. Second, only part of the story is told; namely, the punishment of persecutors. (See reference to standard apocalyptic story order: persecution, followed by punishment of persecutors, followed by salvation of the persecuted on p.6.)

Confirmatory evidence that the trumpet visions foreshadow events which will be described in full when the contents of the scroll are finally declared is provided by the description of complete judgment which accompanies the emptying of the bowls in Chapter 16. This can be seen using a table adapted from Rowland (1993: 82). (See also Lambrecht's similar table 1980: 89–90.)

Trumpets	*Bowls*
8.7 hail and fire mixed with blood; third of earth burnt up.	16.2 evil sores appear on those with mark of Beast.
8.8–9 third of **sea** creatures die after burning mountain thrown into sea and latter is turned into **blood**	16.3 **sea** becomes **blood** and every living thing in it dies.
8.10–11 third of **water** made bitter after star falls from heaven; people die from drinking water.	16.4 **rivers** and **springs** become blood.
8.12 third of **sun** does not shine nor do moon or stars.	16.8–9 humans scorched by **sun**.
9.1–6 air polluted by smoke from abyss after star falls from heaven. Locusts harm humans. Humanity tormented by insects with stings.	16.10 darkness over kingdom of the Beast.
9.13ff. third of humanity killed after the release of the angels bound at the **Euphrates**.	16.12 **Euphrates** dried up to prepare a way for the kings of the east.

To summarize: three major factors suggest that the trumpet visions should be taken as foreshadowings of the contents of the scroll. First, the common association of trumpets (and woes) with announcements. Second, the partial extent of the destruction announced and the omission of a description of the crime which precedes the punishment. Third, the existence of a full description of that which is foreshadowed by the trumpet visions when the bowl judgments are executed in Chapter 16.

The seven thunders: 10.3–4

The seven thunders are unlike the other supposed foreshadowings considered above, in that their contents are not described in the text of Revelation. However, the question of the function of the thunders is worthy of examination here inasmuch as this may prove confirmatory of earlier conclusions and preliminary to the discussion of the function of the little scroll.

An analysis of the function of the thunders incident must begin with the establishment of what the hearers might have expected the thunders to contain if they had been revealed. The majority of scholarly opinion favours the theory that the thunders would have been a further set of limited judgments (e.g. Beckwith 1919: 547–75, 577–8; Farrer 1964: 125; Sweet 1990: 178).

There are three reasons for suggesting that these limited judgments would have served as further foreshadowings of the contents of the scroll if they had been revealed.

First, the thunders are heard in the midst of the sixth trumpet/ second woe (cf. 9.12–11.14). If the trumpet visions are foreshadowings and the thunders fall within one of these visions, then it may be expected that the thunders also foreshadow the scroll's contents.

Second, there is the association of thunder with the imminent arrival of a storm; as Job 36.33 puts it: 'His thunder announces the coming storm.' Thunder could therefore serve as an appropriate indicator of a new set of foreshadowings of disaster.

Third, the angel declares in 10.6–7 that: 'There will be no more delay, but in the days when the seventh angel is to blow his trumpet, the mystery of God will be fulfilled, as he announced to his servants the prophets.' This statement helps to confirm the expectation that all visions seen thus far have constituted a delay, and that the end of this delay will be signalled by the seventh trumpet.

Given the context of the thunders incident, combined with the announcing qualities of thunder, it may be concluded that the thunders would have had the function of foreshadowing the contents of the scroll if they had been recorded.

In the event the sayings of the thunders are sealed. This transforms their function from a further tantalizing set of foreshadowings to a means of confirming that, 'there will be no more delay' (10.6), the precise point at which the delay will be over being in the days of the seventh trumpet.

The little scroll: (10.1–11) 11.1–13

Preliminary notes: Revelation 10.1–11 is included under this title because it is intimately connected with the presentation of the little scroll. However, it is bracketed because it is the contents of the scroll which, it will be argued, should be seen as a foreshadowing. The content of the scroll is seen as beginning at 11.1 because the seer is commanded to prophesy like an Old Testament prophet in 10.11 and immediately starts to speak in the language of Old Testament prophecy in 11.1 (cf. Ezekiel 40). It is taken that Revelation 11.14 (the ending of the second woe) marks a clear break in the text, and so should be seen as the end of the revelation of the contents of the little scroll.

Most ancient commentators took the little scroll to be a description of the witness which would happen before the great and terrible Day of the Lord (cf. Rowland 1993: 99). More recently Bauckham (1993a: 266) has suggested that it directly reveals the contents of the Lamb's scroll, albeit in a nutshell. If this conclusion were correct, then the search for the content of the Lamb's scroll (the story of what must soon take place), would be over. However, careful consideration of Bauckham's evidence reveals that his conclusion is highly questionable.

Bauckham (1993a: 243–5) begins by suggesting that the common designation of 'little' scroll for the scroll of 10.2 is an inconclusive criterion for separating it from the 'main' scroll of 5.1. He follows Mazzaferri (1989: 267–9) in citing evidence for the insignificance of the diminutive in first-century Greek and John's apparent willingness to refer to the scroll as both a *biblaridion* (10.2, 9–10) and a *biblion* (10.8). This section of his argument concludes that: 'This does not show that the scroll of chapter 5 must be the same as the scroll of chapter 10, but it removes the obstacle which has prevented the vast majority of scholars from even considering the possibility' (Bauckham 1993a: 245). In the light of the evidence given it is certainly justified to pursue the question of identity without being hampered by the apparent distinction between *biblion* and *biblaridion*. However, it is still the case that the manuscript evidence (well-attested according to Mazzaferri 1989: 267) leads the printed editions of the Greek New Testament to record the use of the highly unusual term *biblaridion* (the only other occurrence of this term in Greek literature is in the *Shepherd of Hermas* (Bauckham 1993a: 244)) at the crucial first reference to the scroll in 10.2. This first mention is considerably more significant than the subsequent references to the scroll in Chapter 10, since this is the point at which the hearers must decide whether or not to expect the scroll now mentioned to be the same as the scroll of 5.1. The use of a different and highly unusual term favours the perception of a distinction which, once established, need not be mentioned in every subsequent reference to this new scroll.

Bauckham (1993a: 245–57) then presents a series of reasons why the two scrolls should be seen as identical. First, he cites a clear literary link between the mighty angels of 10.1 and 5.2: 'indicating that the account which follows in chapter 10 should be read in close connection with the context of 5.2'. Bauckham admits that this literary connection 'could be taken only to indicate a parallel between the two scrolls, rather than their identity'.

Second, Bauckham suggests Ezekiel 2.8–3.3 as a common source for the scrolls of 5.1 and 10.2 (1993a: 246). His argument proceeds as follows: John is said to notice that a scroll appears in Ezekiel 2.8–3.3 in the context of the inaugural vision of Ezekiel 1.1–3.11. It is noted that this passage contains both a vision of God and a prophetic commission to communicate to the people. The vision of God in Revelation 4.1–11 is said to be: 'considerably indebted to Ezekiel's vision of the divine throne [Ezekiel 1]. Like Ezekiel's vision, this is intended to prepare for the communication of a prophetic message to the prophet. Revelation 5.1 is closely modelled on Ezekiel 2.9–10' (1993a: 246).

Bauckham then goes on to suggest that, while the vision of the scroll in Revelation 5.1 alludes to Ezekiel 2.9–10, the vision of the scroll in Revelation 10 alludes to Ezekiel 3.1–3 (the passage immediately following Ezekiel 2.9–10). He concludes, therefore, that: 'when he closely echoes Ezekiel 3.1–3 in 10.8–10, John clearly still has in mind the description of the scroll in Ezekiel 2.10, which he echoed in 5.1. This strongly suggests that he means to refer to the same scroll in both places' (1993a: 247).

The weakness of Bauckham's argument is the poverty of the supposed parallels between the scroll of Revelation 5.1 and the scroll of Ezekiel 2.9–10. Bauckham seeks to highlight their similarities by placing these two passages side by side:

Ezekiel 2.9–10. I looked, and a hand was stretched out to me, and a written scroll was in it. He spread it before me; it had writing on the front and on the back, and written on it were words of lamentation and mourning and woe.

Revelation 5.1. Then I saw in the right hand of the one seated on the throne a scroll written on the inside and on the back, sealed with seven seals.

In both cases there is a scroll which is written on both sides; both scrolls are also described after a vision of heaven. However, Ezekiel's scroll appears in the context of a commission to prophesy (Ezekiel 2.1–3.11), whereas the scroll of Revelation 5.2 is seen within the context of a heavenly vision devoid of a commission to prophesy. Further, Ezekiel's scroll is open, Revelation's is sealed with seven seals; Ezekiel's scroll is handed to the seer, Revelation's is handed to the Lamb; the content of Ezekiel's scroll is lamentation and mourning and woe, the content of the scroll in Revelation is what must soon take place.

By contrast, a comparison of Ezekiel 2.8–10 and Revelation 10.8–10 reveals three points of similarity.

Ezekiel 2.8–10: 'But you, mortal, hear what I say to you; be not rebellious like that rebellious house; open your mouth, and eat what I give you.' I looked, and a hand was stretched out to me, and a written scroll was in it. He spread it before me; it had writing on the front and on the back, and written on it were words of lamentation and mourning and woe.

Revelation 10.8–10: Then the voice that I had heard from heaven spoke to me again, saying, 'Go, take the scroll that is open in the hand of the angel who is standing on the sea and on the land.' So I went to the angel and told him to give me the little scroll; and he said to me, 'Take it, and eat; it will be bitter in your stomach but as sweet as honey in your mouth.' So I took the little scroll from the hand of the angel and ate it; it was sweet as honey in my mouth, but when I had eaten it, my stomach was made bitter.

First, both prophets are instructed to eat their scrolls (Ezekiel 2.8b and Revelation 10.9). Second, while both scrolls taste sweet initially, both have distasteful consequences (Ezekiel 2.10b; 3.3 and Revelation 10.9b). Third, both scrolls are presented in an open position on an angelic hand (Ezekiel 2.9, 10a and Revelation 10.8).

The only significant difference between these two scrolls is that the scroll in Revelation 10 is not described as double-sided, as Ezekiel's scroll is. However, if John had attributed this detail to the scroll of Revelation 10, then the possibility of confusion with the scroll of Revelation 5 immediately presents itself. The fact that this detail is omitted suggests a deliberate unwillingness to court such confusion.

At this point, therefore, the description of the scroll of Revelation 10 may be seen as alluding to the whole of Ezekiel 2.8–3.3, while there is a lack of evidence to support the theory that the scroll of Revelation 5.1 also alludes to Ezekiel's scroll.

The strength of the connection between the little scroll and Ezekiel's scroll extends into the content of the prophecies (e.g. Ezekiel 4.1–3ff. predicts a siege of Jerusalem and the coming of invaders and Ezekiel 37 predicts the resurrection of Israel), as well as to the act of commission to prophesy. The strength of this connection leads towards the conclusion that John is here re-enacting the prophetic experience of Ezekiel and paraphrasing the contents of his prophecy of the End. If John is indeed playing the role of Ezekiel, then the prophecy he gives cannot be the content of the scroll of Jesus Christ in 5.1. This is the case for two reasons. First, if 11.1–13 represents the revelation *in nuce* of the contents of the scroll of Jesus Christ it is something of an anticlimax, since it reveals nothing new compared to Ezekiel's prophecy. Second, it is highly unlikely that John would see the revelation of the divine Jesus Christ as aping and paraphrasing that of Ezekiel, rather he would see it as expanding and supremely surpassing the earlier revelations of the prophets.

Third, Bauckham (1993a: 248) claims, 'Recognising that the scroll of chapter 10 is the scroll of chapter 5 solves the otherwise insoluble problem of the nature and content of the scroll of chapter 5.' That this problem is not otherwise insoluble will be demonstrated in the remainder of this chapter.

Fourth, Bauckham sees Daniel 12.9 as supplying John with the idea of a *sealed* heavenly scroll which will reveal the meaning of the last things. The allusions to Daniel 12 in Revelation 10 and 11 lead Bauckham (1993a: 252) to conclude that: 'John thought of the scroll of Revelation 10 as a scroll which had been sealed, but has now been opened. It follows that the scroll of Revelation 5.1 is sealed because it is the same scroll.' This reasoning is weak on two counts. First, the acts of sealing and unsealing are not sufficiently uncommon to identify two scrolls as identical. Second, there is an unfounded assumption that John must be taking up the thread left by the idea of Daniel's sealed scroll (Daniel 12.9) when he speaks of a sealed scroll in 5.1. However, this cannot be the case since the revelation of the divine Christ is not something that angels have ever known of and expressed, or that mortals have ever heard (compare Daniel 12.5–9 with Revelation 5.2–5). It is preferable, therefore, to see Revelation 11.1–13 as the revelation of the contents of Daniel's sealed scroll (an event which must take place in the times of the End according to Daniel 12.9), which itself prophesies the contents of the final scroll of Jesus Christ.

Fifth, Bauckham (1993a: 254) argues (following Mazzaferri 1989: 274–8): 'If the scroll the angel brings to John [in 10.2] is the scroll that

John saw in heaven in 5.1–9, we can see that this angel is the angel to whom 1.1 and 22.16 refer.' This is a superficially attractive argument, but Bauckham overstates the case when he says that: 'Only now does it become explicable that, despite the role in communicating the revelation to John which is attributed to Jesus' angel in 1.1 and 22.16, no angel appears as mediating revelation to John until chapter 10.'

This explanation is questionable for two reasons. First, it implies that, because revelation cannot be mediated to John without the angel, the material within 2.1–10.11 is not part of the revelation of Jesus Christ. This assessment does not square with 1.10–20 and 4.1 in which Jesus himself promises direct revelation to John in what follows. Second, the angel in the chain of revelation is designated in 1.1 as, 'his angel' (with reference to Christ). This unique description is preserved, in different forms, on the two other occasions in which the angel in the chain of revelation is mentioned (22.6, 16). The fact that John does not describe the angel of 10.1 in this way suggests that he did not wish these two characters to be seen as identical.

An alternative explanation for the apparent non-appearance of an angel in the process of mediating revelation to John may be provided by equating 'his angel' with the personal messenger of the Godhead: the Spirit. This equation is supported by a curious similarity between the sevenfold spirit (the recognized representation of the Spirit in Revelation, Bauckham 1993b: 110; cf. John's exegesis of Zechariah 4.1–14) and 'his angel'. 'His angel' is always described as belonging to the divinity, but the exact designation is various. In Revelation 1.1 he belongs to Jesus; in 22.6 he belongs to 'The Lord the God of the Spirits'; in 22.16 he belongs to Jesus. This flexibility of ownership is shared by the seven spirits/Spirit. Hence, in 1.4 they are before the throne and so belong to the One on the throne; in 5.6 the seven spirits belong to the Lamb.

If the Spirit may be identified with 'his angel', then this would solve the difficulties mentioned above, at the same time as making good the apparent omission of the Spirit in the revelatory process described in 1.1. Such a making good would fit well with the testimony to the Spirit's revelatory importance as described in 1.10 and 4.1. This would also make sense of the inclusion of the Spirit as one of the divine addressers in 1.4–5 in which it is said, 'Grace to you and peace from him who is and who was and who is to come, and from the seven spirits who are before his throne, and from Jesus Christ the faithful witness...'

A further consideration, of which Bauckham and Mazzaferri fail to take full account, is the fact that the scroll incident is clearly placed within the sixth trumpet blast/second woe (cf. 9.12 and 11.14). The foreshadowing function of the series of seven trumpets creates the expectation that the actual contents of the scroll will be revealed *after* the seventh trumpet has been blown. This supposition is confirmed by the declaration of the angel in 10.6, 7 that: 'there should be no more delay, but that in the days of the trumpet call to be sounded by the seventh angel, the mystery of God, as he announced to his servants the prophets, should be fulfilled.' The introduction of a straightforward revelation of the contents of the scroll before the seventh trumpet blast would therefore create confusion as to whether or not the contents of the scroll were finally being revealed. Such a move would also create destructive ambiguities in the carefully constructed line of tension, which may be expected to extend at least as far as the seventh trumpet blast in 11.15.

So far the evidence in favour of Bauckham's position has been shown to be questionably 'conclusive'. However, in order to refute his conclusion fully it is necessary to present a more convincing account of the function of the little scroll. The alternative suggested here is that the contents of the little scroll foreshadow the contents of the main scroll. Evidence for this position is as follows.

First, the little scroll as a foreshadowing fits within its co-text (the sixth trumpet), and as part of the extended line of tension which leads up to the blowing of the seventh trumpet in 11.15.

Second, the foreshadowing nature of the little scroll is indicated to the hearers by the way in which John takes on the role of an Old Testament prophet (cf. Mazzaferri 1989: 265), and rehearses a paraphrase of apocalyptic prophecy of the past. This prophecy is shown as looking forward to the contents of the scroll of Jesus Christ. It is important for John to show that the Old Testament prophets had an incomplete knowledge of the events of the End, otherwise there would be no need for the revelation of Jesus Christ. At the same time, however, the earlier biblical prophecies must be validated by John, since he clearly sees himself as standing in the same prophetic stream as the earlier prophets. He meets the combined requirement of showing how the prophetic stream is reliable, at the same time as showing that it is incomplete, by presenting the earlier prophecies as pointing forward to, and incompletely foreshadowing, the events contained within the final scroll.

The initial indications that the contents of the little scroll will foreshadow the later revelation of the main scroll are confirmed by the close correlation between the contents of the little scroll (11.1–13) and the visions described in 12.2–14.5 and 16.19 and as follows:

The spiritual protection of God's people: the measuring of the Temple in 11.1 corresponds to the fleeing of the woman to the desert in 12.6, 14. In both cases the image is one of spiritual protection in the face of earthly trials. In both cases the period of protection is 1,260 days (11.3 and 12.6), which coincides with the forty-two months of the Gentiles' power and the reign of the Beast (11.2 and 13.5).

The witness of the faithful: the witness of the two representatives of the kingly and priestly people of God in 11.3–6 corresponds to the witness of the children of the woman in 12.11.

The witnesses conquered by the beast: the beast is seen ascending from the abyss in order to kill the representatives of God's people in 11.7. This corresponds to the beast arising from the sea to conquer those who do not bear his mark in 13.7, 15.

The vindication of the faithful: the glorious raising of the representatives in 11.11–12 corresponds to the vision of the 144,000 in 14.1–5.

The destruction of the city: the fall of the city and the terror of its inhabitants envisaged in 11.13 corresponds to the fall of the city in 16.19.

This remarkably close correlation between the little scroll and the visions of 12.1–14.5 and 16.19 means that it is difficult to see how they can be referring to unrelated events.

In summary: 11.1–13 is not a revelation of the contents of the scroll of 5.1 'in a nutshell', which is later expanded in 12.1ff. Rather, this short scroll is a summary of the veiled and incomplete Old Testament prophetic witness to the contents of the Lamb's scroll. This passage may therefore be seen as a further foreshadowing of the contents of the main scroll.

Summary

The sections of text considered above appear to indicate, in each case, that they should be treated as foreshadowings of the contents of the scroll, rather than as straightforward descriptions of the scroll's contents.

The seal visions (6.1–17) function like a foreshadowing 'table of contents' in which some of the principal elements of the contents of the scroll are sketched in outline.

Before the seventh seal is broken a vision of the people of God before and after the final judgment is shown as a way of illustrating their constant spiritual security. The 'after' picture (7.9–17) may therefore be taken as a form of foreshadowing of events contingent upon the opening of the scroll. This result is ultimately portrayed within 21.1–8.

The trumpet visions (8.2–9.21; 11.14) then maintain suspense by announcing (in such a way as to maintain partial uncertainty about what the exact contents of the scroll will prove to be) what the scroll will eventually be shown to contain. That which the trumpets announce is fulfilled in the bowl visions of 16.1–21.

Embraced within the sixth trumpet vision (9.13–11.14) is the thunders incident (10.3, 4), the preparation of the little scroll (10.1–11) and the revelation of the contents of the little scroll (11.1–13). The little scroll represents a prophecy, in Old Testament style, of what the contents of the main scroll will prove to be, thereby foreshadowing those contents. The vast majority of that which is predicted by the prophetic little scroll is realized in 12.1–14.5.

Figure 1 seeks to illustrate these conclusions. In this diagram the chapter divisions running down the left-hand side are spaced proportionately according to the number of verses in each chapter. The whole text is divided into two halves by the central dotted line. The shaded blocks in the 'foreshadowings' half of the whole correspond to the sections of text considered above. The shaded blocks in the 'direct revelations' half correspond to the principal sections of text within which that which is foreshadowed is directly revealed. The preparation of the contents of the little scroll (10.1–11) (which includes the thunders incident) is unshaded because it does not foreshadow the contents of the main scroll. However, these verses are included with an arrow linking them with the revelation of the contents of the little scroll (11.1–13), to show the preparatory relationship of the former to the latter.

Figure 1 illustrates a concentric arrangement of foreshadowings and direct revelations (cf. Fiorenza's different concentric scheme on p.10). The crafted elegance of this scheme provides confirmatory evidence of the author's intention to use several foreshadowing images to build an ever more detailed, but always incomplete, picture of what the scroll will ultimately prove to contain.

Figure 1 also shows that almost the whole of 6.1–11.14 is concerned with the process of maintaining suspense with respect to the contents of the scroll by foreshadowing those contents. The determination of the

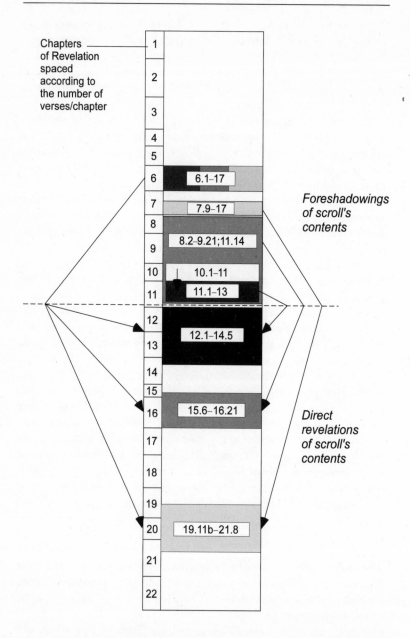

Chapters
of Revelation
spaced
according to
the number of
verses/chapter

*Foreshadowings
of scroll's
contents*

*Direct
revelations
of scroll's
contents*

6.1–17

7.9–17

8.2–9.21;11.14

10.1–11

11.1–13

12.1–14.5

15.6–16.21

19.11b–21.8

Figure 1   The relationship of foreshadowings to the direct revelations of
the contents of the scroll

function of those verses which do not foreshadow the contents of the scroll requires further investigation.

SERIALIZING TEXT

The theory that Revelation was designed to be heard in instalments is suggested by the theatre in which Revelation would originally have been received, a number of aspects of which are uncontroversial. It was clearly designed to be read aloud (1.3) (Bauckham 1993a: 3; A.Y. Collins 1984: 144; Barr 1986: 243). It also appears to have been designed to be read in a congregational setting since it was sent to seven churches (1.11). The fact that the term 'Lord's Day' is used in 1.10 indicates that the text was written after Sunday (from nightfall Saturday to nightfall Sunday) had become the principal day for Christian worship. Saturday night/Sunday daylight is therefore likely to be the time when the congregations would have met to hear the text read. If the text were read at a Sunday service then it may have been accompanied by a Eucharist; the breaking of bread was part of Sunday worship in Paul's ministry (which included at least some of the seven churches) as evidenced in Acts 20.7–11. The possibility that a Communion service was combined with the reading is made more likely by the number of eucharistic references in the text (Barr 1986: 253–5).

The circumstances in which the text would have been read sits uneasily with its length. The whole text takes over two hours to read aloud, even when no Eucharist is added. These circumstances invite the possibility that the text was designed to be read in separate instalments. In order to demonstrate that this was the case it is necessary to provide convincing evidence for the presence of breaks between instalments.

The identification of breaks between instalments

Ideally the textual identification of breaks in Revelation could be carried out by the following process. First, a serialized text of a similar sub-genre would be identified. Second, the characteristics of the breaks in that text would be analysed. Third, similar occurrences of these characteristics would be sought in Revelation.

Unfortunately there are no recognized serialized apocalypses with which Revelation may be compared. This means that it is necessary to analyse the characteristics of breaks in the broader generic category 'serialized narratives'. If Revelation is a serialized text then it will fall within this super-genre and so should exhibit the same characteristics as are common to all texts in this broad genre.

Fortunately there is a characteristic of all serial narratives that is associated with the occurrence of breaks in the narrative. This characteristic is a product of two practical factors common to all performed serialized narratives: the need to persuade the audience to return for the following instalment, and the author's control over where an instalment ends.

These two factors combine to create the need for, and the means of creating, instalment endings which occur at high points of suspense, so that the hearers have to return for the following instalment to find out 'what will happen'. This is the device commonly known as a 'cliffhanger', and it is an almost universal feature of non-concluding instalment endings in performed serial narratives.

The amount of academic literature concerned with the universals of serial narrative is limited. However, all the available evidence supports the thesis that cliffhanging instalment breaks are an intended universal of the genre.

The nineteenth-century revival of serial narrative was led by Charles Dickens with *The Pickwick Papers*. In this first book Dickens confesses in the preface to the 1867 edition: 'experience and study afterwards taught me something, and I could perhaps wish now that these chapters were strung together in a stronger thread of general interest.' Despite the lack of a continuous narrative thread in this early work, Dickens still engineered cliffhanging instalment breaks. For example, at the end of volume one the Stroller is just about to begin his tale when the instalment ends. At the end of volume seven Dickens concludes, 'As this chapter has been a long one however, and as the old man was a remarkable personage, it will be more convenient to us, to let him speak for himself in a fresh one.' Dickens' later works contain more highly developed lines of tension and expertly executed cliffhangers. Other examples of nineteenth-century serial novelists include Trollope and Gaskell.

Jane Austen wrote *Emma* in 1816, before the serial boom, when it was customary to produce novels in two or three volumes which were sold together. Lauritzen (1981: 88) comments on the original version of *Emma*, 'That the three volumes ... are ... constructed so as to include "cliffhangers" that carry over to the following volume.' Lauritzen's book is, however, primarily concerned with the six-part BBC TV adaptation of *Emma*. On page 87 she quotes the adapter, Constanduros. 'The first thing that bothers you always is how to split up the episodes, with a beginning, a middle and an end ... the great thing is always to get climaxes ... and it isn't always easy ... it can be very difficult.' Constanduros goes to great lengths to create suspense at the end of episode 1, drawing together material from six different chapters to create a scene which according to Lauritzen, 'should be provocative enough to attract the audience back for the following episode.'

A link between the generic characteristics of ancient apocalyptic and contemporary science fiction has been noted by Kreuziger (1982). This close connection makes an analysis of a science fiction serial particularly appropriate here. The instalment endings of countless episodes of 'Doctor Who' (BBC TV) exhibit the well-worn, but none the less vital, practice of interrupted suspense at the close of each episode. A brief survey of the instalment endings in *The Masters of Luxor* by Anthony Coburn (1992), should be sufficient to illustrate the point: ending episode 1: Doctor Who and co. sit down to eat a meal which they suspect may be a trap; ending episode 2: Robot explains to Doctor Who and co. that he must suck their life from them in order to give himself life; ending episode 3: with the Doctor's female companions about to be caught and his own life in danger the Doctor sees a sign of hope; ending episode 4: 'The liquid inside the thermometer is slowly but relentlessly rising up the tube towards the danger mark'; ending episode 5: one of Doctor Who's companions is trapped inside the life-sucking machine which has just been switched on to maximum; ending episode 6: the evil planet disappears in a ball of flame.

The above references to 'Doctor Who' may raise the question of whether or not recap pictures are necessary at the beginning of a new episode. This did become a stock feature of 'Doctor Who' (cf. Coburn 1992: 172), but is not a universal of the genre. However, recapping is certainly a common device, and one which is considered with respect to Revelation at several points in the discussion below.

The identification of cliffhangers in Revelation is something of a blunt instrument by which to seek to uncover breaks that have been hidden for many hundreds of years. However, this method provides its own means of refinement as soon as it is applied to the text. Two sections of Revelation are clearly identifiable as perfectly designed to accommodate a cliffhanging instalment ending. A comparative analysis of these two sections will identify common features of structure and content which may then be used as classifying characteristics of instalment breaks which are specific to Revelation. Similar occurrences of these characteristics may then be sought elsewhere in the text.

The first of the two points in Revelation which appear to have been specifically designed to accommodate cliffhanging instalment endings occurs after the breaking of the seventh seal (8.1), and before the issuing of the seven trumpets (8.2). As has already been noted, the breaking of the seventh seal represents a high point of suspense (cf. p.25).

The second point in the text which appears to have been designed to accommodate a cliffhanging instalment ending is after the seventh announcing trumpet has been blown (11.15), and before the full description of the contents of the scroll (12.1ff., cf. p. 6). Suspense regarding the revelation of the contents of the scroll is built up throughout the seal, trumpet and little scroll visions. The imminence of the resolution of this tension is signalled by the last trumpet (11.15, cf. 10.6, 7). Suspense is thus at its peak immediately after the blowing of the seventh trumpet.

Break characteristics arising from a comparative analysis of 8.1–2 and 11.15–12.1

The text and co-text of the two sections of Revelation that have been identified as likely to contain a break between two instalments may now be considered more closely. Eight common features of their structure and content will be noted and discussed as potentially characteristic of instalment breaks in Revelation.

Features common to both sections of text include the following.

1 Suspense

That both sections contain high points of suspense (8.1 and 11.15) has already been noted.

2 The use of derivatives of *anoigo*

A feature common to two verses which stand immediately prior to the release of tension at 8.2 and 12.1 is the use of derivatives of the Greek word *anoigo* meaning 'to open'.

> 8.1   When the Lamb **opened** the seventh seal, there was silence in heaven for about half an hour.

> 11.19   Then God's temple in heaven was **opened**.

The use of *anoigo* at both 8.1 and 12.1 is significant when seen in connection with the opening formula of the whole text. That 1.1 should differ from subsequent opening formulae is to be expected, given its unique relationship to the whole book. However, as the principal opening formula, a relationship with the opening formulae of the subsequent instalments (if they exist) may be expected. Revelation 1.1 speaks of 'apocalypse', which implies a progressive unfolding or making clear of things that are hidden (Beckwith 1919: 417). This process of revealing, promised in the title, is echoed in the images of 'opening' of the heavenly realm found in 8.1 and 11.19. (It should be noted that 8.1 is being suggested as the final verse of one instalment as well as the opening verse of the following one. This overlap may be explained as an example of how a subsequent instalment may begin with a recap picture from the end of the preceding instalment.)

The suitability of these verses as opening formulae, as well as their immediate prior proximity to the resolution of the local tension, indicates that these verses may be taken as likely starting points for two instalments.

3   All action derived from heaven

A reference to all action as being derived from heaven occurs in both 8.1ff. and 11.19ff.

> 8.1   When the Lamb opened the seventh seal, there was silence in **heaven** for about half an hour.

> 11.19   Then God's temple in **heaven** was opened.

These opening pictures reinforce the theology of God's sovereignty, first expressed in 1.1 and more fully developed in 4.2–5.14, in which no action occurs in the universe without first being ordained by the One enthroned in heaven and executed under the authority of the Lamb.

4   Signs of the coming of God

A notable feature of the text that follows the 'opening' formulae of 8.1 and 11.19 is the mention of 'peals of thunder, rumblings, flashes of lightning, and an earthquake' (8.5) and 'flashes of lightning, rumblings, peals of thunder, an earthquake, and heavy hail' (11.19b).

As Bauckham (1993a: 202) notes, 'Earthquakes in the Apocalypse of John play no part in the preliminary judgments. Their role ... is the more traditional Old Testament one of heralding the coming of God in judgment.' This function is suggested by the parallels between these passages and the Sinai theophany (Exodus 19.16, 18) and the development of the significance of this event in later literature where 'the eschatological theophany, the day of the Lord, is clearly portrayed as a new Sinai theophany' (Bauckham 1993a: 200).

The final destination of the story is the coming of God in glory (as stated in 1.4–8). The heraldings of this event in 8.1 and 11.19b represent restatements of that agenda, thus providing an important connection between the content of each instalment and the programme of the whole text. Signs of God's coming may therefore be expected to appear at the start of each instalment.

5   Closing hymns

If the old instalments end at 8.1 and 11.18 then the two sections also share a common use of closing hymnic passages, 7.15–17 and 11.17–18.

In 7.15–17 one of the elders speaks of the martyrs saying:

> For this reason they are before the
>   throne of God,
>   and worship him day and night
>   within his temple;
>   and the one who is seated on
>   the throne will shelter
>   them.
> They will hunger no more, and
>   thirst no more;
>   the sun will not strike them,
>   nor any scorching heat.
> For the Lamb at the centre of the
>   throne will be their
>   shepherd,
>   and he will guide them to
>   springs of the water of life,
> and God will wipe away every
>   tear from their eyes.

In 11.17–18 the twenty-four elders worship God saying:

> We give you thanks, Lord God
>   Almighty,

who are and who were,
for you have taken your great
    power
and begun to reign.
The nations raged,
    but your wrath has come,
    and the time for judging the
        dead,
for rewarding your servants, the
        prophets
    and saints and all who fear your
        name,
    both small and great,
and for destroying those who
        destroy the earth.

The function of the hymnic passages in Revelation has been described as analogous to the role of the chorus in a Greek drama. These interrupt the forward movement of the narrative, serving as a commentary on and preparation for the dramatic moments of the plot (Fiorenza 1985: 166, 171, 172). While these moments of commentary need not only occur in the final verses of a particular instalment their occurrence at clear points of transition would be entirely appropriate.

It is not possible to determine whether or not the congregation would have been expected to join in with these hymns, but presumably this would have been possible once they became familiar with the text (if the songs were not already known as part of the hymnody of the churches). If so, then the hymns provide a means of connecting the world of the text to the world of the hearers, since the hearers, in singing the hymns, would become closely identified with the characters in the text who also sing them.

This process of fusing the world of the text with the world of the hearers is vital to the function of Revelation: the modification of behaviour on the basis of proposed action–consequence relationships. For these action–consequence relationships to have any effect on the behaviour of the hearers it is necessary for the hearers to believe that these consequences apply to their own world as well as to the world of the text. The use of participation at the end of an instalment is one way of encouraging a perception of continuity between the experience of textual characters and of the hearers themselves.

6   Pictures of final outcome

In both cases the instalments end with a picture of the final outcome of the story, 7.9–17 and 11.15–18.

These pictures are an appropriate way of ending instalments, since one of the functions of an apocalypse is the exhortation and consolation of its hearers in the face of real, perceived or expected persecution (Hellholm 1986: 27). As a result the standard story-line of an apocalypse is (a) persecution; (b) punishment of persecutors; (c) reward of the persecuted (A.Y. Collins 1976: 32–44; 1984: 112). If this story-line is serialized, then the consolatory function of the text may be preserved, especially in the early instalments, if the instalment ends on a note of hope and encouragement. This requirement is fulfilled by the use of flash-forward pictures of the final outcome.

7   Eucharistic references

In both cases the closing stages of the instalments use language which may be taken to refer to the Eucharist, especially: 'They will hunger no more and thirst no more', 7.16, and, '*eucharistomen*' (we give you thanks), 11.17 (Barr 1986: 254).

This eucharistic language sits within passages which have a eucharistic tenor in that they point towards the final outcome in which the faithful enjoy full communion with God and the Lamb (21.1–8). The reference to the full communion experience of characters in the text makes a connection with the experience of communion which the hearers would have gone on to enact after hearing the instalment (cf. the practice of following preaching with communion in Acts 20.7–11). This is a means of breaking the boundary of the text to include the experience of the hearers even after reading of the instalment has finished. As a method of creating a continuity between the world of the text and the world of the hearers it is a powerful device, and one which may be expected to characterize the end of each instalment.

8   Instalment length

A further detail about the occurrence of breaks is supplied by the spacing of these two breaks. In the United Bible Societies Third Edition of the Greek New Testament these breaks are 1,728 words apart. This gives some indication of the approximate spacing which may be expected between other breaks.

Identifying further breaks

Having identified eight characteristics common to the verses around two proposed breaks in Revelation it is now possible to identify where these characteristics occur elsewhere in the text in similar groups of verses.

Break after 3.22

The most compelling reason for identifying a break after 3.22 is on the basis of the universally recognized difference between the form of 1.1–3.22 and 4.1ff. This distinct difference in form between the text before and after 3.22 makes it likely that a break occurs here if there are breaks in the text. At the same time this difference in form makes exact subscription to the criteria for breaks, established above, unlikely, especially with respect to material prior to the break. However, a number of the above criteria are still satisfied.

1   Suspense

The cliffhanging device is not achieved by the establishment of one large element of suspense; instead it is created by seven smaller tensions which are all focused on the advent of 4.1ff. This suspense may be expressed for each congregation in the question: 'What is going to happen to *us* soon?'

2   The use of a derivative of *anoigo*

An opening formula which includes a use of *anoigo* occurs in 4.1.

> After this I looked, and there in heaven a door stood **open**! And the first voice, which I had heard speaking to me like a trumpet, said, 'Come up here, and I will show you what must take place after this.'

3   All action derived from heaven

The full development of the theology of God's sovereignty, visually expressed by the derivation of all action from heaven, is described from 4.1–5.14, and continues to pervade the whole of the text.

4   Sign of the coming of God

A close parallel to the signs of God's coming in 8.5 and 11.19b may be found in 4.5.

4.5   lightning, rumblings and thunder.

8.5   thunder, rumblings, lightning and earthquake.

11.19   lightning, rumblings, thunder, earthquake and heavy hail.

These three heraldings of God's coming as judge (Bauckham 1993a: 199–202) find their initial realization in the final bowl judgment where a similar, but expanded, formula appears:

16.18–21 lightning, rumblings, thunder, a violent earthquake, islands flee, no mountains found and great hailstones fall.

Hence, there are three stages in the process of God's arrival on earth. Its announcement in heaven (the progressive opening formulae), its announcement on earth (the disasters of 16.18–21), and its full realization on earth (20.11–21.8).

5 Closing hymn

There is no hymnic material which may be seen as directly parallel to the closing hymns of 7.15–17 or 11.17–18. However, there are seven short reflective/preparatory refrains which accompany each of the seven messages (2.7, 11, 17, 29; 3.5, 12, 21).

6 Picture of final outcome

There is no single picture of final outcome as in 7.9–17 or 11.15–18. Instead there are seven smaller pictures of final outcome, one to accompany each of the seven messages (2.7, 10, 17, 26–28; 3.5, 12, 21).

7 Eucharistic references

There is more than one eucharistic reference. The conquerors at Ephesus are told they will eat of the tree of life (2.7), and those at Pergamum are promised the hidden manna (2.17). However, the clearest eucharistic reference does come at the end of the instalment in the letter to the church at Laodicea: 'I will come in to you and eat with you, and you with me' (3.20).

8 Instalment length

A break after 3.22 creates a first instalment of 1,811 words (1.1–3.22). The second instalment would then be 1,620 words (4.1–8.1).

In summary, a break after 3.22 exhibits all the classifying characteristics established above. That some of these occur in a different form may be accounted for as a consequence of the differences of form between 1.1–3.22 and 4.1ff.

Break after 8.1

See above, pp. 38–42.

Break after 11.18

See above, pp. 38–42.

Break after 15.4

1   Suspense

Suspense is created by a series of announcements that begin at 14.6. The first angel announces the hour of God's judgment on his enemies (14.6–7). The second angel proleptically announces the fall of Babylon (14.8). The third angel uses the future tense to announce the doom of those who bear the mark of the beast, the persecutors of God's people (14.9–11). These warnings of the coming judgment of the persecutors are then followed by an exhortation to the saints to escape this coming judgment by remaining faithful (14.12), for which they will in due course receive their reward (14.13). So far there has been clear announcement of the coming judgment, but the punishments announced do not actually occur until 16.1–21.

The harvesters of 14.14–20 prepare to harvest and the ripeness of the time for harvesting is emphasized, thus further building the expectation that the full description of the judgment of God's enemies is imminent. The fact that the harvesters actually put in their sickles suggests that judgment is enacted at this point. That this is not the case is indicated by the brevity with which the judgment is described. This implies that a full description must be imminent after the first-fruits have been gathered (cf. 19.15).

A final element of suspense is supplied by the initial vision of the seven angels with the seven plagues (15.1). These are described as the final judgment and represent the consummation of the judgments which were foreshadowed earlier in the text, especially in the trumpet visions.

All these elements of suspense are resolved when the angels reappear in 15.5 and enact the final judgments. (The introduction of an instalment break between 15.1 and 15.5 helps to explain the otherwise curious repetition of the appearance of the plague angels. In this case 15.5 serves as a recap picture.) 15.4 therefore represents a suitable point of tension, immediately prior to resolution of that tension, at which to locate an instalment break.

2 The use of a derivative of *anoigo*

An opening formula which includes a use of *anoigo* occurs in 15.5.

> After this I looked, and temple of the tent of witness in heaven was **opened**.

3 All action derived from heaven

Revelation 15.5 begins in heaven, see above, and all subsequent action in the instalment flows from this vision.

4 Sign of the coming of God

The signs of the coming of God have, thus far, used elements of the Sinai theophany as a means of heralding God's coming as judge and king. The appearance of smoke in the temple (15.8) represents a further example of the use of Exodus 19 in this way.

> On the morning of the third day there was thunder and lightning, as well as a thick cloud on the mountain, and a blast of a trumpet so loud that all the people who were in the camp trembled.... Now Mount Sinai was wrapped in smoke, because the Lord had descended upon it in fire; the smoke went up like the smoke from a kiln, while the whole mountain shook violently.
>
> (Exodus 19.16, 18)

5 Closing hymn

A closing hymn is sung – the conquerors sing the song of Moses in 15.3–4:

> Great and amazing are you
> deeds,
> Lord God the Almighty!
> Just and true are your ways,

King of the nations!
Lord, who will not fear
and glorify your name?
For you alone are holy.
All nations will come
and worship before you,
for your judgments have been
revealed.

6   Picture of final outcome

A picture of the final outcome is shown in 15.2–4.

7   Eucharistic reference

There is eucharistic significance in the harvest of the first-fruits of the wheat and the vines (14.14–20). Because these crops are harvested they become available, in the imagination of the hearers, for the bread and wine of the Eucharist. Thus the text makes a connection between the judgment and salvation enacted in the text and the judgment and salvation enacted in the eating of the bread and the drinking of the wine at the hearers' Communion.

8   Instalment length

A break after 15.4 creates a fourth instalment of 1,729 words (11.19–15.4).

Break after 19.10

1   Suspense

The suspense prior to this final break has two elements. The first is that created by the announcement made in 16.13–16, that the foul spirits have gone out to gather all the kings of the whole world for the final battle at Harmagedon. Since it is the kings of the world who are God's agents of Babylon's destruction (17.17), together with the beast of 17.12, they are still at large after this destruction and a further battle will be necessary to defeat them. This battle does not occur before the proposed break at 19.10 and so it must be expected in the following instalment.

The second element of suspense does not need elaborate preparation. The faithful hearers have received promises of reward in the initial letters and at the end of every instalment. Now that the judgment of Babylon has been achieved (16.2–14) the hearers can expect that the long-awaited vision of eternal reward will soon be described in full. This expectation gives the appearance of being fulfilled when in 19.6 the multitude announce the arrival of the marriage supper of the Lamb. However, after a short coda, which includes the blessing of those who are invited to this supper, the instalment comes to an end before this reward is fully described.

2 The use of a derivative of *anoigo*

An opening formula which includes a use of *anoigo* occurs in 19.11.

> Then I saw heaven **opened**, and there was a white horse. Its rider is called Faithful and True.

3 All action derived from heaven

The heavenly initiation of the following action is made clear in the opening verse, see 19.11 above, in which the messianic rider is seen riding from heaven.

4 Sign of the coming of God

By this stage in the story the progress of God's coming from his throne (4.5) to reign and judge on earth (20.11–15) is nearly over. The picture of the messianic rider on the white horse (19.11) fits within the series of signs which lead through the opening sequences of each instalment towards this end point.

5 Closing hymn

A closing hymn occurs in 19.6–8 after the extended hymnic passage beginning at 18.1 – the multitude in heaven sing:

> Hallelujah!
> For the Lord our God
>   the Almighty reigns.
> Let us rejoice and exult
>   and give him the glory,
> for the marriage of the Lamb has
>   come,

and his Bride has made herself
ready;
to her it has been granted to be
clothed
with fine linen, bright and
pure.

6   Picture of final outcome

A picture of the final outcome is provided in 19.6–9, in which God's undisputed reign and the marriage of Christ with his people is anticipated.

7   Eucharistic reference

The announcement of the marriage supper of the Lamb (19.7) and the blessing of those who are invited to share in it (19.9) provide a suitable lead in to the hearers' earthly, foreshadowing experience of that supper, their own eucharistic celebration.

8   Instalment length

A break after 19.10 creates a fifth instalment of 2,055 words (15.5–19.10), and a sixth instalment of 1,928 words (19.11–22.21).

Table 1 (p.50) summarizes the occurrence of all the classifying characteristics for each of the breaks considered above.

The beginning and end of the text

In considering Table 1 it should be noted that only non-concluding instalment breaks are considered. There are two other breaks: before the text starts and when it is finally completed. By virtue of their specific function these two breaks are unique in many respects; however, there are important areas of conformity with the intermediate breaks in areas where this is possible.

1   Suspense

The instalment that ends at 22.21 closes with the most sophisticated suspension in the whole text. Within 6.1–11.18 the device of foreshadowing had been used to create suspense. This suspense was

Table 1: Criteria for the identification of breaks between instalments

	3.22	**8.1 (re-opening at 8.1)**
Suspense at end of instalment	Must wait for description of 'what must soon take place'	Must wait for scroll's contents (now unsealed)
Use of '*anoigo*'	4.1 After this I looked, and there in heaven a door stood open	8.1 When the Lamb opened the seventh seal...
Action derived from heaven	4.1ff.	8.1ff.
Signs of the coming of God	4.5 Lightning, rumblings, thunder	8.5 Thunder, rumblings, lightning, earthquake
Closing hymn	2.7, 11, 17, 29; 3.6, 13, 22	7.15–17
Final outcome picture	2.7, 10, 17, 26–28; 3.5, 12, 21.	7.9–17
Eucharistic reference	2.7, 17; 3.20	7.16
Length: (1.1–3.22) 1,811 words	(4.1–8.1) 1,620 words	(8.1–11.18) 1,728 words

then resolved within the story in the course of instalments 4, 5 and 6. However, as the hearers approach the end of instalment 6 (22.6ff.), they are reminded that the story itself is a foreshadowing (the seventh trumpet/third woe) of what will happen when the story unfolds in reality.

Prior to each of the previous four breaks the hearers have been left with a suspense picture: the scroll just opened, the final trumpet blowing, the plague angels poised with their plagues, the Bride awaiting the Bridegroom. At the end of the sixth instalment the suspense picture is of Christ declaring that he is coming soon (21.7, 17, 20).

The absence of a seventh written instalment means that the resolution of this tension transfers fully to the world of the hearers and out of the world of the text. The two worlds become one and the author's objective in this respect is fully achieved. The determination of some commentators (e.g. Palmer (1988) and A.Y. Collins) to force the text into a pattern of seven sevens denies this effect.

11.18	15.4	19.10
Must wait for scroll's contents (no more announcements)	Must wait for bowls to be emptied	Must wait for Harmagedon and messianic supper
11.19 Then God's temple in heaven was opened,...	15.5 After this ... the temple of the tent of witness in heaven was opened	19.11 Then I saw heaven opened
11.19ff.	15.5ff.	19.11ff.
11.19 Lightning, rumblings, thunder, earthquake, hail	15.8 Smoke fills the temple	19.11 The messianic rider arrives
11.17–18	15.3–4	19.6–8
11.15–18	15.2–4	19.6–9
11.17	14.14–20	19.7, 9
(11.19–15.4) 1,729 words	(15.5–19.10) 2,055 words	(19.11–22.21) 1,928 words

2   The opening formula

The relationship of the principal opening formula to its subordinates has already been mentioned above (pp.39–40). Now that each of the opening formulae have been identified the overall pattern of this relationship may be seen a little more clearly. To recap, 1.1 speaks of an *Apokalupsis*, which implies a progressive unveiling of heavenly things. This process of unfolding is echoed in the use of progressive 'openings' into heaven, unique to the proposed opening formulae of the subsequent instalments: 4.1, John enters heaven through an open door; 8.1, the seventh seal is opened and new activity in heaven is revealed; 11.19, the temple in heaven is opened; 15.5, the temple of the tent of witness in heaven is opened; 19.11, John sees heaven standing wide open.

3   All action derived from heaven

The action begins in heaven, as with the other instalments. God's sovereignty is established from the start. All that is to be revealed comes from God, only Jesus Christ is able to reveal it/set it in motion (1.1). All the other players are described as responding to this divine initiation of the action, they take no action of their own accord.

4   Sign of the coming of God

The sign of the coming of God appears in 1.4–8. This is an extremely important passage with respect to the whole book, in that here the theophanic/Christophanic agenda of the whole story is set out. All the signs of God's coming at the start of subsequent instalments, and elsewhere (e.g. 16.18, 21), trace the progress of this programme. From God enthroned in glory in 4.5, through the increasing intensity of the signs of his coming in 8.5; 11.19; 15.8, to the preparatory acts of his coming 16.18, 21, to his Christophanic arrival in 19.11 and complete arrival in 20.11–21.8.

5   Closing hymn

There is no closing hymn. However, an interactive liturgy is possible at 22.17:

Reader: The Spirit and the bride say, 'Come'. And let everyone who hears say.
Hearers: 'Come!'

Also in 22.20:

Reader: Surely I am coming soon.
Hearers: Amen. Come, Lord Jesus!

6   Picture of final outcome

This is unnecessary in view of the picture of final outcome that is supplied within the story element of this instalment (19.11–21.8).

7   Eucharistic reference

There are a number of eucharistic references in the closing stages of the text. These include the references to the water of life (22.1, 17), the

marriage of the Lamb to his Bride (21.17) and the invitation of the
Lord to come (22.17, 20) (cf. 'maranatha' in *Didache*, Chapter 10; Barr
1986: 254).

Conclusion

In the course of identifying breaks between instalments certain sections
of text have been shown to have the function of opening and closing
the various instalments, and, in the later instalments, of creating suspense by means of direct announcement (this function is performed by
the foreshadowings in earlier instalments). Hence, at least one of the
functions of the following sections has now been accounted for.

4.1	opening formula
7.9–8.1	closing formula
8.1	opening formula
11.15–18	closing formula
11.19	opening formula
14.6–15.4	suspense creation and closing formula
15.5	opening formula
19.6–10	suspense creation and closing formula
19.11a	opening formula
22.6–21	epilogue, suspense creation and closure

FURTHER SUPPORTING TEXT

PERSUADING HEARERS OF THE RELEVANCE OF THE WHOLE TEXT

Revelation 1.1–3.22 has the function of convincing the hearers that the
revelation which they are about to hear is worth listening to. (This is a
factor which remains as a constant throughout the hearing of the
revelation.) Various reasons are given.

The authority of the author

The revelation is declared to be that of Jesus Christ which God gave
him (1.1). The authoritative and divine nature of the addresser is then
expanded upon in the epistolary prescript and doxology (1.4b–8), in the
commissary vision (1.13–20) and at the opening of each of the seven
messages (2.1, 8, 12, 18; 3.1, 7, 14). There is also an appeal to the

divine authority of the addresser in the repeated exhortation to hear what the Spirit has to say to the churches (2.7, 11, 17, 29; 3.6, 13, 22).

If these claims of divine authorship are to be believed then there can be little doubt that this is a text worth listening to. However, any audience must take 'John's' word that this is indeed the source of his text. This means that the authority of the text rests not so much in the authority of the Godhead, but in the reliability and authority of the seer and on the likelihood that he would have been chosen to communicate such revelations. This raises the subject of John's identity.

External evidence of John's identity

In his *Dialogue with Trypho*, written around AD 135, Justin Martyr, a sometime resident of Ephesus, attributes Revelation to John, one of the apostles of Christ. In *Against Heresies*, written about AD 180, Irenaeus attributes Revelation and the Fourth Gospel to the apostle John. Later authors, including Hippolytus, Tertullian, Clement of Alexandria and Origen, follow this lead and attribute the Apocalypse to John the apostle. As Mounce concludes: 'It cannot be disputed that the Apocalypse was widely accepted by the second-century church as the work of John the apostle' (1977: 29).

The history of the authorship debate from the second century onwards includes a number of false assumptions and unnecessary complications. If these may be left aside, then the only question in debate is whether or not Justin and Irenaeus are reliable witnesses.

Those who seek to discredit these witnesses tend to focus on Irenaeus. He is a softer target because of his attribution, unlike Justin, of both the Fourth Gospel and Revelation to John the apostle. This has been considered an unlikely conclusion since the third century, when Dionysius, disturbed by the way in which Revelation was being used by opponents in his diocese, sought to discredit the book by comparing it with the Gospel and Epistles. Differences in language, style and eschatology led him to conclude that they could not have been written by the same author. At the time this observation was used to 'prove' that because John wrote the Fourth Gospel he could not have written Revelation. (This argument still exerts a remarkable influence in the debate, despite the fact that it relies on the over-confident assumption of the Fourth Gospel's Johannine authorship.) Even though Dionysius' observation does not necessarily lead to the conclusion which he drew, it does throw doubt on the reliability of Irenaeus' witness, because of the latter's seemingly false claim that both works were written by John.

Before Irenaeus is discarded as an unreliable witness the possibility of common authorship for the Fourth Gospel and Revelation should be considered in the light of the new understanding of the structure of Revelation, described above.

The principal reasons for assuming different authors for the Gospel and Revelation have been a discontinuity in the language and eschatology of the two works. Charles (1920: cxxi) notes that: 'While the Greek of the Gospel is relatively simple and normally correct, the Apocalypse seems to pay little attention to the basic laws of concord'. On the question of eschatology the difference is expressed by Mounce: 'While the eschatological focus of the Apocalypse is on a time yet future in which God will bring salvation, the Gospel is concerned with an eschatology that has already been "realized" in the present age' (1977: 30).

The new understanding of the structure of Revelation throws light on both of these issues. First, the eschatology of Revelation is revealed to be more 'realized' than has previously been recognized. That is to say that, although the hearers are promised the full experience of the messianic feast in the End (e.g. 19.9), they are invited to experience a present foretaste of that feast in their experience of the eucharistic celebration which follows each instalment.

The second important obstacle to common authorship would be removed if it were possible to demonstrate that the material from which John's Gospel was composed had originally been in the form of a serial narrative designed to form part of a eucharistic service. That this is possible is suggested by the repetitive structure of John's Gospel and its regular allusions to eucharistic themes (e.g. the wedding at Cana, water of life, bread of life, the passion narrative, the post-resurrection meal by the Sea of Tiberias, cf. Cullmann 1953). If this original text was later redacted to produce a continuous narrative, then this may account for the differences of style between Revelation and John's Gospel. That there has been some redaction of the disciple's original written text after his death is suggested by John 21.23, 24, 'So the rumour spread in the community that this disciple would not die. Yet Jesus did not say to him that he would not die. ... This is the disciple who is testifying to these things and has written them, and we know that his testimony is true.'

It is not within the scope of this study to present a complete argument for the common authorship of Revelation and the Fourth Gospel. This requires much more detailed research (Mounce 1977: 30). However, this new evidence re-opens the possibility that the apostle John was the common authority behind both texts. In these circumstances

the out-of-hand rejection of Irenaeus' testimony to Johannine authorship is unjustified.

Returning to Justin's testimony, Collins attempts to discredit Justin
by associating him with Irenaeus' supposed inaccuracies regarding
common authorship. She says: 'A second, more critical look at Irenaeus
supports the conclusion that he, *and probably Justin as well*, was mistaken in this matter' (A.Y. Collins 1984: 29, emphasis added). Even if
Irenaeus' testimony were discredited (for which there is less justi-
fication than there at first appears), this is no reason to disregard
Justin's earlier testimony. Collins' inclusion of Justin as she draws
her conclusions regarding Irenaeus shows that she has no good
reason to disregard Justin. Therefore, with Irenaeus' testimony given
new credibility and Justin's evidence maintained, the external
evidence should be seen as favouring the apostle John as author of
Revelation.

Internal evidence of John's identity

The authority of an apocalyptic text is vital to its success. It is all
very well for someone to claim that they have received a revelation
from God, but that chain of revelation is only as strong as its
weakest link. This explains why most apocalypses claim to have been
written by some great and authoritative figure from the past (e.g.
Abraham, Enoch, Baruch, Ezra, etc.). This is not the case with Revelation. Here the author describes himself simply as 'John', a fellow
servant with his brothers the prophets. This humble designation suggests that the author of Revelation was someone whose personal
authority was beyond question. In this respect John's authority
surpasses even that of the apostle Paul, who often had to restate the
basis of his authority (e.g. Galatians 1.1). This kind of automatic
authority is more likely to have been enjoyed by an apostle than a
non-apostle.

Collins presents a powerful argument against apostolic authorship
when she points out that 21.14 refers to the names of the twelve
apostles being written on the foundations of the holy city. 'This saying
reflects a situation in which the time of the apostles is past. It is unlikely
that a living apostle would speak in such a way' (A.Y. Collins 1984: 27).
This is a good argument for suggesting the post-apostolic date of this
verse. However, a number of factors suggest that this verse, along with
the two other verses which describe the foundations (21.19–20), may be
later additions to the original text.

The first clue to the possibility that 21.14, 19–20 are late additions is a variation between the significance of the term 'apostle' in 21.14 and in 2.2. In Revelation 2.2 the Ephesian church is congratulated for testing so-called apostles. This suggests that this verse was written during a period when apostles were still active (cf. 2 Corinthians 11.13). The reference to the apostles in 21.14, on the other hand, presents them as characters of the past, the foundations of the Church rather than its current leaders.

A consideration of the relationship of 21.14, 19–20 to the other verses in the passage 21.9–21 provides further evidence of their later addition. First, this passage does not suffer in terms of sense or structure if these verses are removed:

> Then one of the seven angels who had the seven bowls full of the seven last plagues came and said to me, 'Come and I will show you the Bride, the wife of the Lamb.' And in the Spirit he carried me away to a great, high mountain, and showed me the holy city Jerusalem coming down out of heaven from God. It has the glory of God, and a radiance like a very rare jewel, like jasper, clear as crystal. It has a great, high wall, with twelve gates, and at the gates twelve angels, and on the gates are inscribed the names of the twelve tribes of the Israelites; on the east three gates, on the north three gates, on the south three gates and on the west three gates. [21.14 omitted] The angel who talked to me had a measuring rod of gold to measure the city and its gates and walls. The city lies foursquare, its length the same as its width; and he measured the city with his rod, fifteen hundred miles; its length and width and height are equal. He also measured its wall, one hundred forty-four cubits by human measurement, which the angel was using. The wall is built of jasper, while the city is pure gold, clear as glass. [21.19–20 omitted] And the twelve gates are twelve pearls, each of the gates is a single pearl, and the street of the city is pure gold, transparent as glass.

In fact the omission of these verses significantly improves, rather than damages, the structure and sense of this passage. This improvement is particularly noticeable in the case of the omission of 21.19–20. The heading for this paragraph (21.15) mentions the measuring of the city, its gates and walls. When 21.19–20 are removed these three features are described in a uniform manner (as above) with refrains that refer back to the clear and golden nature of the city (21.18, 21). The insertion of 21.19–20, however, interrupts this threefold programme with a description of the foundations. Furthermore, the style and content of this interruption is different from the way in which the other features of the city are described. For example, the city, walls and gates are all described as being made of a single material. The description of the foundations, on the other hand, only mentions the variety of materials with which they are adorned.

The visual symmetry of the city is also confused by the inclusion of foundations. The geometric shape of the city, a perfect cube (21.16), is unbalanced by the addition of protruding foundations. Also the aesthetic unity of the city, which, in its golden, translucent quality resembles a single gem (21.11), is disturbed by the introduction of multi-coloured foundations which are encrusted with twelve different types of precious stone.

The principal argument against the suggestion that 21.14, 19–20 are later additions is the absence of any manuscript evidence which suggests this possibility. However, this may be accounted for by considering the likely motivation for these additions. The bride in Revelation is the heavenly counterpart of the earthly church and so the omission of the foundational role of the apostles could have been seen as an oversight which it was legitimate to remedy. This sentiment could have arisen from an early date, leading to an early emendation. This would account for the absence of manuscript evidence to support the theory that 21.14, 19–20 are later additions.

Arguments for authorship which depend on the exclusion of unwanted verses as late additions should always be treated with extreme caution. However, the combination of factors outlined above leads me to conclude that the likely late date of 21.14 should not be seen as providing a solid basis for non-apostolic authorship of the whole text.

Conclusion

There is no good reason to disregard Justin's early attestation of the apostle John as the author of Revelation. Irenaeus' testimony is more questionable, but even here the substance of his witness may prove to be more accurate than has been assumed in recent centuries.

The internal evidence consists of John's low-key presentation of himself, despite the need to ensure that his authority is recognized. This suggests that 'John' had a personal authority consistent with his being the apostle. The post-apostolic presentation of the apostles, as foundations of the New Jerusalem (21.14, 19–20), militates against apostolic authorship. However, two pieces of evidence suggest that these verses are later additions to the original text. First, the late use of the term 'apostle', compared to the early use of this term in 2.2. Second, the disruption which the addition of these verses causes to the sense and structure of 21.9–21.

It is therefore concluded that the preponderance of external and internal evidence favours the identification of 'John' as John the apostle. This conclusion enhances the authority of the whole text and therefore increases the likelihood that its hearers would have considered the text worthy of their attention.

The specificity of the intended audience

For the congregations of the seven churches there could have been no doubt that the revelation was for them – it could not be ignored as applying to someone else (1.11, 20; 2.1, 8, 12, 18; 3.1, 7, 14). The absolute applicability of the revelation to these congregations is further emphasized by the addresser's apparent knowledge of each of the churches' situations (2.2–4, 9, 13–15, 19–20; 3.1b–2, 8, 15–17; see Hemer 1986).

The consequences of listening and not listening

Those who hear the revelation and obey it are described as 'blessed' in 1.3. The particular nature of this blessing is indicated at the end of each of the messages (2.7b, 10b–11, 17, 26–29; 3.5, 10–13, 20–21). Conversely, the punishment for failure to hear and obey is indicated in 2.4–5, 14–16, 20–23; 3.1b–3, 15–19, for those churches where punishment is applicable.

The immediacy with which the events described are expected to take place

The expected continuity of the present situation with the events predicted for the future is made clear in 1.1, 3; 1.19; 3.11. Given this urgency the revelation must be listened to and acted upon immediately.

In summary, the whole of 1.1–3.22 may be said to have the function of securing the hearers' attention. This is achieved by virtue of the authority of the addresser, the specificity of the addressees and the contents of the message (cf. 1.1a).

ESTABLISHING THE CONTINUOUS SOVEREIGNTY OF GOD AND THE LAMB

The function of 4.2–5.14 is clearly not to tell the story, since no action on earth (in the experience of the earthly characters) takes place in this passage. Rather, the function of this section is to establish that throughout all that follows God is sovereign.

4.2–5.14 may be characterized as a description of the control-room of the universe. In it the supreme deity is seen as the enthroned focus of worship for every living thing in heaven, on earth, under the earth and in the sea; everything that is (4.1–11; 5.13–14).

Within this overall sovereignty the Lamb is depicted as having specific control over the contents of the scroll (5.1–12, cf. also 6.1, 3, 5 etc.). His unique worthiness to open the scroll implies that consequences that follow the scroll's unsealing all flow from the sole and uncompromised will of the Lamb.

ESTABLISHING THE CONTINUOUS SPIRITUAL SECURITY OF GOD'S PEOPLE

Before the scroll begins to be unsealed three constants have been established: that the text is worth listening to, that God is sovereign over all and that all action in the story derives from the will and action of the Lamb.

While the latter two constants are of some comfort to the intended hearers, they leave one important question unanswered. As the first six seals are removed this question becomes increasingly urgent, 'Is there any difference between the fate of the just and the unjust?' This question is answered just before the final seal is broken and the judgments inside the scroll may be expected to be unleashed. A space is created in the action (7.1) and the people of God are sealed with God's seal. This appears to indicate spiritual security (see also 11.1 and 12.6, 16). The way in which the people of God are pictured as ancient tribes of Israel is reminiscent of God's spiritual preservation at the Passover in Exodus; the picture of the redeemed in final bliss which immediately follows indicates that this seal of spiritual security remains throughout all that follows. This too, therefore, represents a constant feature which applies throughout the rest of the text (see also p. 21).

REVIEWING AND INTERPRETING TEXTS

17.1–18 and 21.9–22.5 are two passages which have been recognized as having the function of commenting on and interpreting events which immediately precede them in the narrative (Giblin 1991: 159, 196). This function is clearly indicated in both cases by the use of an interpreting angel (17.1, 21.9). In both cases the angel offers to show the seer that which has just been described (17.1b, 21.9b)

A further passage, similar to the others in that it is backward-looking, is 18.1–19.5 which represents a hymnic response to the judgment which has preceded it.

None of these assessments of function is contentious; it is only necessary to mention them in order to clarify that these three passages are not concerned with straightforward story-telling.

STORY-TELLING TEXT

The function of every section of text in Revelation has been accounted for, with the exception of 12.1–14.5; 15.6–16.21; 19.11b–21.8. Each of these passages may be identified as describing the story contained within the main scroll.

That the contents of the scroll begin to be revealed at some point after 11.15 is indicated by the build-up of foreshadowings culminating in the blowing of the last trumpet (11.15, cf. 10.6). As has already been discussed, the verses which immediately follow 11.15 (11.15b–18) have the function of closing the instalment, while 11.19 opens the instalment which follows. 12.1 therefore represents the first opportunity for the contents of the scroll to be revealed.

The events that ensue after 12.1 continue in sequential order until 14.6. At this point the three angels interpose to announce what will take place in the following instalment. It may therefore be concluded that the first block of story-telling text extends from 12.1–14.5.

The announcements of judgment which begin at 14.6 culminate in the appearance of the seven angels (15.1), who will complete that which has been predicted up until this point by the seal visions, trumpet visions, little scroll, announcing angels and first-fruit harvesters. The actual description of their acts is deferred while the instalment is closed (15.2–4) and the following instalment is opened (15.5), then straightforward action is described from 15.6.

The description of judgment which begins at 15.6 continues until 16.21. Then in 17.1 there is a transition to a passage which interprets the events of the previous chapter. It may therefore be concluded that the second block of story-telling text extends from 15.6–16.21.

The whole text of Revelation points towards the coming of God in glory (cf. 1.7 and progressive signs of theophany in the opening formulae). Revelation 19.7 and 19.9 intimate that this event is imminent. It is realized, after the instalment has been closed and the following instalment re-opened, with the vision of the rider of the white horse. Revelation 19.11b may therefore be taken as the start of the text which describes the final events recorded in the scroll.

The events which follow 19.11b develop in sequence until 21.9, where the commentating angel (cf. 17.1), interposes to review and interpret the foregoing visions. It may therefore be concluded that the third block of story-telling text extends from 19.11b–21.8.

SUMMARY OF FUNCTIONS IN REVELATION

1.1–3	Title, addresser, addressees (relevance to hearers)
1.4–20	Prologue (relevance to hearers)
2.1–3.22	Messages (relevance to hearers)
4.1	Door in heaven opened (opening formula)
4.2–11	Worship of God as Creator (constant – sovereignty)
5.1–14	Worship of Lamb as worthy to open the scroll (constant – sovereignty)
6.1–17	The first six seals removed and accompanying visions (foreshadowing)
7.1–8	The preservation of God's people prior to the onslaught (constant – security)
7.9–17	Flash-forward to the reward of the conquerors (foreshadowing constant – security and closing formula)
8.1	Opening of the seventh seal (opening formula)
8.2–11.14	First six trumpets announce judgments (foreshadowing)
10.1–11.13	The little scroll (foreshadowing)
11.15a	Seventh trumpet (signals the end of foreshadowings)
11.15b–18	Vision of final judgment and reward (announcement and closing formula)
11.19	Temple opened (opening formula)
12.1–14.5	Explanation for, and description of, persecution (story-telling)
14.6–20	Announcement of impending judgment (announcement)

| 15.1 | The agents of final judgment are previewed (announcement) |
| 15.2–4 | Response to judgment and salvation (announcement and closing formula) |

15.5	Temple of tent of witness opened (opening formula)
15.6–16.21	The seven bowls of judgment (story-telling)
17.1–18	Commentary on bowl judgments (interpretation)
18.1–19.5	Responses to the vision of judgment (review)
19.6–10	Song in which marriage supper announced (announcement and closing formula)

19.11a	Heaven standing open (opening formula)
19.11b–20.3	Rider defeats Beast and False Prophet; Satan is bound (story-telling)
20.4–6	The Martyrs rule with Christ (story-telling)
20.7–10	Satan and remaining enemies defeated (story-telling)
20.11–15	The Final Judgement (story-telling)
21.1–8	God's complete rule is established (story-telling)
21.9–22.5	Commentary on New Order (interpretation)
22.6–21	Epilogue (announcement and final closing formula)

A pictorial representation of this structure (Figure 2) omits some of the detail of the version above, but serves to illustrate the way in which the text emphasizes the importance of the three story-telling passages. (Garrow (1994: 66–73) provides further structural diagrams which illustrate the occurrence, in each of the instalments, of the three story elements: persecution of Christians, punishment of persecutors, salvation of the persecuted.)

CONCLUSION

At the beginning of this chapter it was noted that Revelation claims to reveal the story of 'what must soon take place' and that this story is contained within the main scroll. By means of an analysis of the different functions performed by each section of text it has been possible to identify the overall structure of the text, locate three story-telling passages within that structure and establish the functional relationship of the rest of the text to these three passages.

At this stage it would be possible to examine the story-telling passages (in the knowledge that some passages foreshadow these sections,

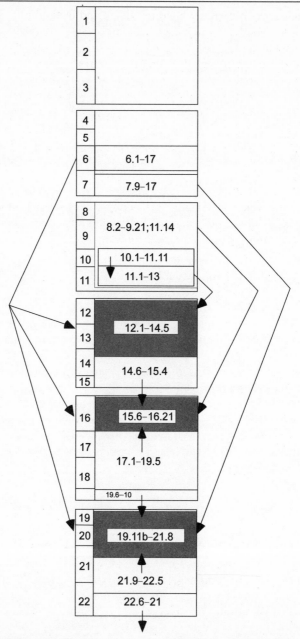

Figure 2 The identification of story-telling passages in Revelation and their relationship to other parts of the text

while others retrospectively interpret them), and demonstrate that the characters therein perform a coherent sequence of actions with respect to one another. The presentation of this abstract story would provide useful confirmation of the structural theory presented in this chapter; however, this would reveal little or nothing of the meaning of this story for John's intended hearers. Such an exercise would be analogous to studying an ancient political cartoon strip without knowledge of the circumstances on which the cartoonist was commenting; even though the images in the cartoon may perform a series of logical and connected actions, these images are meaningless when taken out of context.

The next stage of this reading, therefore, must be to consider the situation to which Revelation was addressed. Hence, the following chapter will consider the dating of Revelation, a first step towards the apprehension of the text's historical context.

Chapter 4

Locating the story in history

Knowledge of the date at which Revelation was written is of course vital to the study of the historical context in which it was designed to be interpreted. Unfortunately, most of the evidence for date is so ambiguous that a wide variety of different dates may be entertained. The two most popular possibilities are *c.* AD 95 and AD 68. The strengths and weaknesses of these two dates will now be considered. This will be followed by an argument for an alternative date of *c.* AD 80.

THE DOMITIANIC DATE: *c.* AD 95

The argument for a Domitianic date is founded on the tradition, derived from Irenaeus, that John's Revelation was seen 'towards the end of Domitian's reign'. Three factors have commonly been seen as defending Irenaeus' testimony: reports of Domitian's demand for divine worship, a supposed persecution of Christians under him, and his edict of AD 92 to cut down vines in Asia Minor. Other minor pieces of evidence have been seen as supporting a Domitianic date (e.g. Hemer 1986: 2–5), but these are all ambiguous and may not be seen as providing a case for a Domitianic date independent of the more important pieces of evidence listed above. In order to test the validity of the Domitianic date, therefore, it is necessary to test the strength of Irenaeus' testimony and of the three further factors which appear to support this date.

Irenaeus' testimony

Irenaeus claims that John's Revelation was seen, 'no very long time since, but almost in our own day, towards the end of Domitian's reign'

(*Against Heresies* 5.30.3). Domitian reigned from AD 81–96 and so Irenaeus has been taken as dating Revelation to *c*. AD 95.

Reasonable doubt may be cast over Irenaeus' testimony in the first instance because, as Moberly points out, 'Irenaeus was writing in Gaul, during the AD 180s or late AD 170s, about when an apocalyptic vision had been seen in Patmos.... He thinks that John saw it 80–95 sketchily charted years earlier – in other words 35 sketchily charted years, or so, before he [Irenaeus] was born. We would not normally regard so distant, belated and second-hand an opinion as, by itself, evidence' (Moberly 1992: 367, 381 quoted in Court 1994: 96).

The second cause for doubt arises from a recognition that Irenaeus' testimony occurs in a text entitled *A refutation of knowledge falsely so called* (commonly known as *Against Heresies*, hereafter *A.H.*). This title implies that Irenaeus' motivation for dating Revelation was to win an argument against his Gnostic opponents, rather than to record a historical fact. It need not be the case that there was a conflict between a persuasive date and an accurate date; however, the possibility that such a conflict does exist is worthy of further investigation. This requires the consideration of an outline of the particular argument in which Irenaeus' date for Revelation occurs.

In *A.H.* 5.30. 1–3 Irenaeus seeks to make two points. First, that the number of the beast is 666 rather than 616 (a number apparently proposed by his Gnostic opponents). Second, that, prior to the arrival of the ten kings, speculation as to the identity of the Antichrist may not be pronounced upon positively.

It is the second of these two points which is of primary interest here, since it is in the course of this part of his argument (*A.H.* 5.30.3), that Irenaeus records his date for Revelation. The following represents a brief outline of the development of this argument:

Statement of objective: to persuade opponents to wait for the fulfilment of prophecy rather than speculating as to the identity of the Antichrist.

Point 1: speculation is fruitless. Many names fit the number, but none can be proved correct, so the problem of identity is unsolved.

Illustration of Point 1: three names are considered. Despite the merits of 'Titan' it is not possible to pronounce positively that this is the name of the Antichrist.

Point 2: speculation is not intended. If the author had wanted the name of the Antichrist to be known he would have announced it.

Supplement to Point 2: the time for identification has not yet arrived. The name was 'not announced' fairly recently (towards the end of Domitian's reign), and so this lack of announcement still holds good.

The expressed motive for dating Revelation to *c.* AD 95 is to suggest that the non-interpretation of the name behind the number still holds good for his own times (*c.* AD 180).

Another significant motivation for providing this dating remains unstated. In order to appreciate this motive it is necessary to note Irenaeus' reliance on his supposed access to the witness of those, notably Polycarp, who saw the apostles 'face to face' and who knew John personally. The martyrdom of Polycarp, aged 85, most commonly dated to *c.* AD 166–7 (Eusebius, *Historia Ecclesiastica* 4.15.6; Frend 1965: 270), would make him approximately sixteen years old in AD 95. That *c.* AD 95 represents the beginning of Polycarp's acquaintance with John is suggested by Irenaeus' emphasis on his witnesses' contact with John in Trajan's reign (*A.H.* 2.22.5 and 3.3.4). The lack of references to events in John's life prior to the end of Domitian's reign also suggests that Irenaeus' witnesses do not predate this point.

If Irenaeus' claimed witnesses only extend as far back as *c.* AD 95, then an unstated motive for dating Revelation to this time may be suggested. If Irenaeus had allowed for the possibility that Revelation was written earlier than *c.* AD 95, then his opponents could have claimed knowledge of an interpretation of the number of the beast which predated that which could have been passed on to Irenaeus by his witnesses. In an attempt to close off this possibility Irenaeus claims that there was little or no gap between the arrival of Revelation and his witnesses contact with it. Hence, Irenaeus claims, the name behind the number has *never* been known.

The fact that Irenaeus had motives for dating Revelation to *c.* AD 95 does not necessarily mean that this is an inaccurate date, but his claim that the name behind the number has never been known does provoke strong suspicion. This claim appears to contradict the expectation of the text that those who are wise will be able to understand the meaning of the number (13.18). The level of wisdom required does not appear to be high; the other puzzle which invites the wise to understand it is very simple (17.9). It is therefore necessary to decide which of the following statements is least likely to be true, since all three cannot co-exist.

1 The name is decipherable (Revelation 13.18).
2 The text was written in *c.* AD 95 (Irenaeus *A.H.* 5.30.3).

3 Irenaeus' witnesses, presumably present at *c.* AD 95 (implied by Irenaeus), did not know the name behind the number (*A.H.* 5.30.3).

The first of these three statements is highly likely to be correct (cf. pp. 84–6). If the second is true, then the third may be untrue for two reasons. The first possibility is that Irenaeus' witnesses did not exist or were not present in *c.* AD 95; in which case Irenaeus' date should be disregarded altogether. The second possibility is that they knew the date and the name behind the number, but communicated only the date and withheld the name. This is not an impossible scenario but it stretches the bounds of credibility. Of the options therefore, it is most likely, either, that both the second and third statements are untrue, or, that the third is true and the second is a fiction created by Irenaeus to support his argument.

A further anomaly occurs in Irenaeus' discussion of the variant reading 616 instead of 666. In the course of this passage he claims to have access to 'ancient and approved copies' (*A.H.* 5.30.1) of Revelation. This may be a rhetorical device, but this description of his sources sits uneasily with his claim that the revelation was seen 'almost in our own day' (*A.H.* 5.30.3).

In entertaining the possibility that Irenaeus' date is inaccurate, it is not necessary to suggest that he deliberately recorded an inaccurate date in the sense that he knew the correct date but recorded a false one. Instead it is more likely that Irenaeus combined two traditions: that of his witnesses' contact with the apostle John, and that of their familiarity with Revelation. It would be natural enough for Irenaeus to assume that his witnesses were present when Revelation was first heard, especially when such a convergence was so convenient for his argument.

Domitian's demand for divine worship

Domitian's supposed demand to be always addressed as 'Lord and God' (Suetonius, *Domitian* 13.2) has often been seen as providing a suitable context for Revelation (e.g. Beasley-Murray 1978: 38; Caird 1984: 6). However, Thompson (1990: 95–116, especially 104–7) demonstrates that there is no record of Domitian being addressed as 'Lord and God' in any official documents, contemporary with his reign. In the same passage Thompson argues convincingly that Domitian's divine pretensions were a construct of Trajan's historians, designed to condemn Domitian. Thompson concludes:

The presence of the imperial cult, especially in Asia Minor is not here being questioned; it had been a significant force in the social life of the Asian province from the time of Augustus. There is no indication, however, that Domitian modified the imperial cult by demanding greater divine honours than either his predecessors or successors.

(Thompson 1990: 107)

Therefore, Domitian's reign provides no more suitable a context for Revelation than that of any other emperor.

Domitianic persecution

Irenaeus' date of *c.* AD 95 has been thought to provide a plausible setting for Revelation because of the evidence of a Domitianic persecution of Christians (Beasley-Murray 1978: 38). However, the lack of evidence for a Domitianic persecution makes this argument untenable (A.Y. Collins 1984: 56, 69–73, 77; Thompson 1990: 95–167 especially 167). Confusingly, the *lack* of evidence for a Domitianic persecution is used by Collins and Thompson to support Irenaeus' date on the grounds that Revelation addressed a situation in which persecution is expected (2.10; 3.10; 6.11), but not yet widely experienced (1.9; 2.13). In the absence of evidence that Domitian entertained extraordinary divine pretensions (see above), there is little reason to see why John should have had a greater expectation of imminent persecution in *c.* AD 95, than at any other time in the preceding forty years.

Domitian's edict of AD 92

The injunction to the third rider (Revelation 6.5–6) to spare the oil and the wine, has been thought by some (e.g. Court 1979: 59–60; Hemer 1986: 4) to refer to a decree made by Domitian in AD 92 to cut down Asian vines in order to promote grain cultivation (Suetonius, *Domitian* 7.2; 14.2). A link between this edict and Revelation 6.6 is tenuous because the edict makes no reference to olive trees. It is therefore more likely that the third rider is a symbol of conventional warfare, an unwritten rule of which was that olives and vines should not be damaged by an invading army (cf. Hemer 1986: 265). The poverty of the correlation of 6.6 to the Domitianic edict, and the alternative explanation for the inclusion of this image in Revelation, means that this verse may not be used to tie the text to a Domitianic date.

The prophecy of the seven kings

The most important piece of evidence against a date of *c.* AD 95 is the prophecy of the seven kings in Revelation 17.10. This prophecy states that, 'The seven heads [of the beast] are ... seven kings, five of whom have fallen, one is, the other has not yet come'. The ruler list from Julius Caesar to Domitian is as follows (see also the Appendix):

Julius Caesar (dictator)
Augustus (emperor; as all following)
Tiberius
Gaius (Caligula)
Claudius
Nero
Galba
Otho
Vitellius
Vespasian
Titus
Domitian

In order to make Domitian the emperor who 'is' at the time of writing it is necessary to entertain one of the following systems. The most obvious would be to start the counting at Galba, but this cannot be correct because this would require the omission of Nero, and all the evidence points to Nero being the most important head of the seven (cf. pp.84-7). Another alternative, therefore, is to omit the short-lived emperors Galba, Otho and Vitellius. If this were allowed, then the counting could begin at Caligula (A.Y. Collins 1984: 64). However, the text gives no encouragement to make these omissions, for which there is no precedent in contemporary literature (Bell 1979: 99). It may not even be argued that the rapid succession of these rulers would have been of little significance to the people of Asia Minor, since the history of the year in which they reigned was a well-known and tumultuous landmark in the life of the whole empire (Josephus, *The Jewish War* iv.496). (Bauckham (1993a: 443) describes this year as making a 'deep impression on those who lived through it', and quotes occasions in the contemporary literature where these events are recalled.) Scholars who favour a Domitianic date, but who admit that the king list cannot be made to fit Domitian's reign satisfactorily, must claim a merely symbolic significance for the number seven (Caird 1984: 218–19; Sweet 1990: 257). For example, Caird suggests that: 'The seven kings are a symbolic number, representative of the whole series of emperors, and they would remain seven no matter how long the actual list happened to be.' Three points suggest that this is a convenient fudge. First, seven kings which are purely symbolic sit uncomfortably alongside the adjacent reference to the symbolic and literal seven hills of Rome (17.9). Second, there is no evidence that king lists are used in this kind of purely symbolic fashion in any other piece of apocalyptic literature (Robinson 1976: 245–7). Third, the function of 17.10 is not only to indicate when the beast will return, but also when it first arose (cf. p.77), so in order for this calculation to be made with accuracy the length of the list must be specific and static. In summary then, the prophecy of the seven kings may only be made to support a Domitianic date if it is manipulated in ways which are not justified by the contemporary literature, or by the text itself. Therefore, the evidence for date provided by the prophecy of the seven kings weighs heavily against a Domitianic date.

Conclusion

The veracity of Irenaeus' testimony is subject to reasonable doubt for four reasons. First, Irenaeus' distance from the text means that we would not normally consider his testimony as firm evidence. Second, Irenaeus was arguing and not recording and so, in the absence of a precise tradition regarding date, Irenaeus is likely to have chosen that date which best supported his argument. Third, two internal inconsistencies in Irenaeus' argument would be resolved if Revelation were actually written at an earlier date. Fourth, Irenaeus' date is not specifically or independently supported by any other piece of internal or external evidence and is contradicted by the most important element of that evidence, the prophecy of the seven kings. The principal pieces of evidence which have traditionally been taken as supportive of Irenaeus' testimony have been undermined to such an extent that they are no longer sufficiently substantial to do so. In these circumstances conclusions regarding the date of Revelation should be reserved until the evidence for alternative dates has been considered.

THE YEAR OF THE FOUR EMPERORS: AD 68–9

Scholars who favour an early date for Revelation base their case on two main pieces of evidence. First, the prophecy of the seven kings. Second, the reference to the temple in 11.1, 2.

The prophecy of the seven kings

The most explicit piece of evidence for AD 68–9, is that provided by the prophecy of the seven kings in Revelation 17.10. Here it is stated that five kings have fallen, one is, the other has not yet come. If these kings could be counted, then it might be expected that the ruling emperor at the time of writing would be revealed.

If counting begins with Julius Caesar, then Nero is the sixth emperor. However, the text implies that Nero is a past emperor because he is the best candidate for the beast who was, is not and is to come (17.11) (cf. pp.84–6). This means that counting should begin with Augustus at the earliest. This could be a logical starting point from the perspective of Asia Minor, since Pergamum was the first city to receive a licence to worship a living Roman ruler, Augustus, in 29 BC. This practice soon spread throughout the rest of the region (Hemer 1986: 84). Counting from Augustus, then, the sixth emperor is Galba, who reigned in AD 68–9, hence the dating to this period.

The presence of the temple

Some scholars take the presence of a standing temple in Revelation 11.1, 2 as evidence that the temple in Jerusalem had not fallen at the time of writing (Robinson 1976: 238–42). The strength of this case may be assessed after undertaking a brief exegesis of 11.1–13.

The prophecy begins with a command to measure the temple of God, the altar and those who worship there. The act of measuring is one which symbolizes the making secure of these areas and the people within them. This securing act is therefore parallel to the sealing of God's faithful people (7.3) and the safety of the woman in the wilderness (12.6, 14).

In contrast the court outside the temple is left unmeasured and exposed to the trampling of the nations. This may be taken as symbolizing the physical exposure of God's people despite their spiritual security.

The two witnesses then prophesy throughout the period during which the outer court is trampled (11.3–6). These witnesses perform a parallel function to that performed by the children of the woman in 12.11, 17. Hence, it may be concluded that they symbolize the faithful people of God, preserved for witness in the temple.

When the beast ascends from the bottomless pit to conquer and kill the witnesses (11.7), they are described as lying 'in the street of the great city which is prophetically called Sodom and Egypt, where their Lord was crucified' (11.8). The reference to the location of Christ's crucifixion has led some scholars to see the 'great city' as Jerusalem. However, this conclusion is unlikely in the light of the clear indication that the description of the city is prophetic or allegorical, rather than a literal one. Further, on the seven other occasions where the term 'the great city' is used (16.19; 17.18; 18.10, 16, 18, 19, 21), the city referred to is Rome (Caird 1984: 138). The idea that Jesus died in Rome is unproblematic in that he died at the hands of a Roman governor in the province of Judea, an extension of Rome's city limits. The point about the city is, however, not its geographical location, but its spiritual status as the place where evil held sway. For John the location of beastly power had been Rome, and there is no difficulty in seeing both Christ and the Christian martyrs as falling victim to the same power, and so in the same spiritual location.

Ultimately the witnesses, like Christ, are raised and ascend to join the army of heaven (11.11, 12). In response to their ascent, a tenth of the city falls, seven thousand people are killed and the remainder are terrified and give glory to God (11.13). The falling of a tenth of the city is an indication of the ultimate fate of Rome in that this tenth is a first-fruit, or tithe, which prefigures the full and final destruction of the city. The connection between the exaltation of the martyrs and the destruction of the city and its population implies that the full complement of martyrs (cf. 6.11) will bring about the total destruction of the city.

Returning to the question of whether or not the temple in Jerusalem had fallen at the time of writing, it may be observed from the above exegesis that the whole focus of this prophecy is on the fate of the faithful followers of Christ, their spiritual security, witness, martyrdom and final vindication. John could not have written this prophecy before the fall of the temple since to do so would have invited the possible identification of the Jerusalem temple as the place preserved by God, and its Jewish inhabitants as exemplars of God's faithful witnesses whose Lord was crucified. This association is unlikely enough on its own, even without the recollection of John's assessment of the Jews as a 'synagogue of Satan' (2.9; 3.9).

While there is a potential for the confusion of imagery if 11.1–13 was written before AD 70, this is not the case if it were written after the fall of the temple. In this circumstance John's clear allusion to the fall of the temple enables him to keep faith with the important place of these events in the earlier eschatological predictions of Ezekiel, Daniel and Jesus (Mark 13). However, he re-invents the significance of these predictions by presenting them as references to the challenges which face the 'true' temple, Christ's Church. The 'true' status of this new temple is emphasized by contrasting its fate with that of the old temple. The perpetual spiritual security of the new temple (signifying God's presence) is contrasted with the desecration of the old temple (signifying God's abandonment) (Josephus, *The Jewish War* vi.260–6). The ministry to the world of the two witnesses is contrasted with the infighting of the Simon and John factions in the last days of Jerusalem (Josephus, *The Jewish War* v.248–57). The glorious vindication of the Christian martyrs and the terror of the citizens of the city is contrasted with the terror of the Jerusalem Jews and the glory achieved by Titus.

In summary, if 11.1–13 were written before AD 70, then it could be seen as casting the Jews of Jerusalem as perfect exemplars of God's faithful people. This is highly unlikely to be John's intention in the light of his description of the Jews as a synagogue of Satan in 2.9 and 3.9. It is therefore preferable to suppose that the prophecy was written after AD 70.

Babylon

The term 'Babylon' is used to describe Rome in 4 Ezra 3–14, 2 Baruch and the fifth book of *Sibylline Oracles*. A.Y. Collins (1984: 57–8) notes that: 'In each case where it occurs in these three works, the context makes it abundantly clear why the name Babylon was chosen. Rome is called Babylon because her forces, like those of Babylon at an earlier time, destroyed the temple and Jerusalem.' Collins therefore concludes that, 'It is highly unlikely that the name would have been used before the destruction of the temple by Titus.' Even if John saw the Roman persecution of Christians in AD 65 (Tacitus, *Annals* 15.44) as the true fall of the temple, then his desire to compare and contrast this event with the fall of the Jerusalem temple means that his use of the term 'Babylon' is unlikely to predate this Jewish description of Rome.

Conclusion

The strongest piece of evidence which supports a date of AD 68–9 is the prophecy of the seven kings. However, no other piece of evidence, despite first appearances, may be taken as corroborating this date. The prophecy of the seven kings may be otherwise believably interpreted (see below), and so it is concluded that the case for a date of AD 68–9 is sufficiently weak to fuel the search for a more convincing date.

TITUS: AD 79–81

Revelation is seldom dated to the reign of Titus. Sweet (1990: 256) suggests this date as the simplest solution to the puzzle of the seven kings (see below), but rejects this possibility because it conflicts with Irenaeus' testimony. However, the weakness of Irenaeus' testimony, discussed above, brings the Titus date back into contention.

The prophecy of the seven kings

In Revelation 17.10, John says, 'This calls for a mind that has wisdom: The seven heads [of the beast] are ... seven kings, of whom five have fallen, one is living, and the other has not yet come.'

Before assessing the contribution of this passage to the date debate it is necessary to consider two preliminary questions. First, the nature of the relationship between the kings of the text and the emperors of history; second, the function of 17.9–10.

Several indicators suggest that the prophecy refers to seven historical emperors. First, and most generally, one of the major functions of apocalyptic literature is to explain how present events are in continuity with God's overall plan, despite apparent evidence to the contrary. The seer achieves this function by reporting the hearers' situation from a heavenly perspective and revealing how God's sovereign plan will be accomplished. While these reports may be couched in symbolic language it is important that they are recognizable to the hearers as referring to actual events and persons in their world (Robinson 1976: 245–7). Second, two features of the text encourage a direct association between real emperors and the kings of the text. First, the call for wisdom invites a particular calculation to be made (cf. 13.18). Second, the seven mountains of 17.9 refer to the seven literal hills of Rome. It is therefore likely, in the absence of any indication to the contrary, that the seven kings refer to seven historical emperors. The acceptance of a direct relationship between the seven kings and seven actual Roman emperors does not necessarily imply that they are seven consecutive rulers. However, there is no indication that this is not the case and so it may be expected that the intended hearers would have made their calculation of the identity of the beast on the basis that five consecutive kings had fallen, and that the one who is to come would immediately follow the one who is. Some scholars have suggested that only certain emperors should be selected (e.g. A.Y. Collins 1984: 59–60). This approach is not justified by the presence of any selection criteria in the text, nor is there any precedent for a selective king list in any other contemporary literature, apocalyptic or otherwise (Bell 1979: 99). It is therefore concluded that the seven kings of 17.10 refer to seven historical, consecutive emperors.

The function of 17.9–10 is the second preliminary question. The function of these verses is most often commented on in the negative. That is to say that scholars tend to observe that the function of these verses is not to reveal the date of the text, since the hearers would already been aware of this (Sweet 1990: 255; Bauckham 1993a: 406). While this is a valid point it is one which does not recognize the value of the actual function of 17.9–10 in the date debate. The function of 17.9–10 is to confirm/reveal the identity of the beast. This function is implied by the context, in which an angel promises to explain the mystery of the beast, and also by the phrase: 'This calls for a mind that has wisdom'. This latter formula echoes 13.18: 'This calls for wisdom: let anyone with understanding calculate the number of the beast, for it is the number of a person. Its number is six hundred and sixty-six'. There can be little doubt that the function of 13.18 is to reveal/confirm the identity of the beast, and so 17.9–10 may be seen as having a similar function.

Having considered these preliminary points, 17.9–10 may be considered from the hearers' point of view. From the formula, 'this calls for a mind that has wisdom', they are invited to identify the kings which comprise the heads of the beast. To do this they must count back five kings (and forward one before the eighth' who is one of the seven, returns). This calculation may be represented thus:

present emperor − four emperors = first emperor of the beast

This equation may be re-ordered thus:

first emperor of the beast + four emperors = present emperor

Thus, if the emperor whose arrival coincided with the appearance of the beast may be identified, then the date of writing is revealed. It is argued on pp.84–7 that Nero's first reign represented the first appearance of the beast. Hence, the equation may be written thus:

Nero + four emperors = present emperor

The four emperors who followed Nero were Galba, Otho, Vitellius and Vespasian. The next in the sequence is Titus. Hence, by this calculation, Titus was the reigning emperor at the time of writing.

Vesuvius

It has already been noted that the seal visions appear to make veiled allusions to real events in the hearers' past so as to suggest that these earthly disasters were reflections of the heavenly consequences of the unsealing process (pp.18–19). This practice has the effect, not only of merging the world of the hearers and the world of the text, but also of creating a sense of the imminence of the Final things. That is to say, on first hearing the text the audience would have assumed that the revelation of the contents of the scroll would immediately follow the breaking of the seventh seal. If the sixth seal vision appeared to refer to a recent calamitous event, then this would heighten the expectation that the Final events were imminent, not only in the text, but also in reality. The sixth seal vision portrays a cataclysm whose proportions it is difficult to associate with reality; however, a real event which could have been seen as mirroring this vision was the eruption of Vesuvius in AD 79. This eruption was reported by Suetonius (*Titus* 8) as one of several unprecedented disasters which occurred in Titus' reign, and is described as immediately preceding the return of Nero in *Sibylline Oracles* 4.130–6. If the sixth seal vision does allude to the eruption of Vesuvius, then Revelation must have been written after AD 79.

Conclusion

Revelation may be dated to the reign of Titus (hereafter *c*. AD 80) for the following reasons. First, and most importantly, Nero is identified as the first head of the beast, so that Titus is the emperor 'who is', according to the prophecy of the seven kings (17.10). Second, the sixth seal vision may allude to the eruption of Vesuvius and so sets an earliest possible date of AD 79.

SUMMARY CONCLUSION

Irenaeus' testimony provides the crucial evidence for the most popular date for Revelation: *c*. AD 95. However, this testimony has been shown to be of dubious reliability, since it was motivated by the need to clinch an argument, rather than to record an accurate date for posterity. Furthermore, it has been shown that Irenaeus' date is in conflict with the most important piece of internal evidence – the prophecy of the seven kings in 17.10. The principal alternative date of AD 68–9 has been shown to do greater justice to the evidence provided by the prophecy of the seven kings. However, indications within the text that the Jerusalem temple had fallen at the time of writing, and the presence of the term 'Babylon' to describe Rome, suggest that this early date should also be discounted. A reconsideration of the significance of the prophecy of the seven kings, taking into account its function as a means of identifying the beast, has led to the ultimate conclusion that Revelation was written during the reign of Titus (*c.* AD 80).

THE SIGNIFICANCE OF A DATE OF *c.* AD 80

The dating of Revelation to *c.* AD 80 affects the interpretation of the book inasmuch as this date places the text at a time when the Nero *redivivus* myth was current in Asia Minor. The first of the impostors who claimed to be Nero appeared soon after his death in AD 69. The second 'false Nero' arose in AD 80 and is described by Bauckham (1993a: 413) in the following way: 'He appeared in the province of Asia Minor, where he acquired a few followers, but he gained far more followers as he marched east towards the Euphrates. There he won the support of Artapanus IV, a pretender to the Parthian throne who supported him against the emperor Titus presumably because of the latter's refusal to back his own claim. It is not known how the matter ended.' Three other noteworthy features of the historical context of John's hearers in *c.* AD 80 include the relatively recent persecution of Christians in Rome under Nero in AD 65, the stability of the Roman empire under the popular leadership of Titus, and the growth of friction between Christians and Jews. The significance of these features of historical context for the interpretation and purpose of the story will be considered in the following two chapters.

Chapter 5

Interpreting the story

In Chapter 3, 'Finding the story in the text', it was concluded that the story is contained within the main scroll and that this scroll's contents are revealed in 12.1–14.5; 15.6–16.21; 19.11b–21.8. Other parts of the text were identified as foreshadowing and reviewing these sections of story-telling text. With the benefit of this understanding of the structure of the text, and an awareness of the importance of the Nero myth in the environment of John's hearers, it is possible to interpret John's perception of 'what must soon take place' for his intended hearers.

The story begins with an explanation of the background to persecution which does not strictly fit within the bracket of 'what must soon take place' but rather of 'what is, and what is to take place after this' (1.19).

REVELATION 12.1–6

[12.1] A great portent appeared in heaven: a woman clothed with the sun, with the moon under her feet, and on her head a crown of twelve stars. [12.2] She was pregnant and was crying out in birth-pangs, in the agony of giving birth. [12.3] Then another portent appeared in heaven: a great red dragon, with seven heads and ten horns, and seven diadems on his head. [12.4] His tail swept down a third of the stars of heaven and threw them to the earth. The dragon stood before the woman who was about to bear a child, so that he might devour her child as soon as it was born. [12.5] And she gave birth to a son, a male child, who is to rule all the nations with a rod of iron. But her child was snatched away and taken to God and to his throne; [12.6] and the woman fled into the wilderness, where she has a place prepared by God, so that there she can be nourished for one thousand two hundred and sixty days.

Characters

Caird (1984: 149) states: 'The woman clothed with the sun is the mother of the Messiah, not Mary, but the messianic community' (see also, Mounce 1977: 236; Sweet 1990: 195; Swete 1907: 148). The woman's later career also identifies her as the spiritual dimension of God's faithful people (see comments on 12.13–16 below).

The dragon/Satan/serpent/accuser of the brethren/devil (12.3–17; 13.2, 4; 20.2–3, 7–10) are all titles for the leader of the forces opposed to God. For simplicity's sake this character will usually be called Satan in the following discussion.

The child of the woman (12.5) is the Christ, also described as the Lamb in 5.6f. and 12.11.

Action

As Christ appears, Satan seeks to destroy him (12.4), both through the temptations of his life but supremely in the cross (Caird 1984: 150). In the act of martyrdom Christ is snatched up to heaven and to God's throne (12.5). Assuming that this passage speaks of the life, death and resurrection of the earthly Jesus, then Satan, whose centre of operations is in heaven (12.7), works through the human agency of Rome to attack the earthly Jesus. However, an alternative interpretation is possible in that these images may be seen as referring to the heavenly events which led to Satan's original fall from heaven (cf. Beckwith 1919: 617). In this case these images would refer to the life, death and resurrection of Jesus only inasmuch as events in heaven were believed to have their counterpart on earth. Whichever of these possibilities is actually the case the result as far as the story is concerned is the same – Christ is victorious through martyrdom (cf. 12.11).

REVELATION 12.7–12

[12.7] And war broke out in heaven; Michael and his angels fought against the dragon. The dragon and his angels fought back, [12.8] but they were defeated, and there was no longer any place for them in heaven. [12.9] The great dragon was thrown down, that ancient serpent, who is called Devil and Satan, the deceiver of the whole world – he was thrown down to the earth, and his angels were thrown down with him. [12.10] Then I heard a loud voice in heaven, proclaiming,

'Now have come the salvation and the power and the kingdom of
our God and the authority of his Messiah, for the accuser of our
comrades has been thrown down, who accuses them day and
night before our God. [12.11] But they have conquered him by
the blood of the Lamb and by the word of their testimony, for they
did not cling to life even in the face of death. [12.12] Rejoice then,
you heavens and those who dwell in them! But woe to the earth
and the sea, for the devil has come down to you with great wrath,
because he knows that his time is short!'

Characters

Michael is an archangel and leader of the heavenly host (cf. Daniel
10.13, 21; 12.1 and Jude 9). Michael appears in this leadership role,
rather than Christ, so that the complete destruction of Satan may be
accomplished by Christ in the closing stages of the story (20.10).

Action

Christ's martyrdom and exaltation to God's throne enables the armies
of heaven to cast Satan and his armies out of heaven (12.7–9). Revelation 12.10–12 reflects on these events and looks forward to their
consequences. In 12.10 a voice from heaven declares that Christ's reign
in heaven is unchallenged now that the accuser of Christians on earth
has been thrown down. In 12.11 the voice implies (although it speaks
proleptically) that in the next phase of the on-going battle, Christians
on earth will defeat Satan by the same means that Christ defeated him,
namely, martyrdom. The voice concludes (12.12) by restating the
supremacy of Christ in heaven, but warning of the coming tribulation
on earth.

REVELATION 12.13–16

[12.13] So when the dragon saw that he had been thrown down
to the earth, he pursued the woman who had given birth to the
male child. [12.14] But the woman was given the two wings of the
great eagle, so that she could fly from the serpent into the wilderness,
to her place where she is nourished for a time, and times, and half
a time. [12.15] Then from his mouth, the serpent poured water like
a river after the woman, to sweep her away with the flood. [12.16]
But the earth came to the help of the woman; it opened its

mouth and swallowed the river that the dragon had poured from his
mouth.

Action

Having been cast out of heaven Satan's attention turns to the earthly
members of God's kingdom. He begins by making an attack on the
messianic community (12.13). However, she escapes to the desert which
is a place of spiritual security for the duration of the period of tribulation (cf. 7.1–17; 11.1, 2).

REVELATION 12.17, 18

[12.17] Then the dragon was angry with the woman, and went off to
make war on the rest of her children, those who keep the command-
ments of God and hold the testimony of Jesus. [12.18] Then the
dragon took his stand on the sand of the seashore.

Characters

The children of the woman represent the physical and insecure dimension of God's faithful people. The woman in the desert (12.14–16) is
preserved like the temple of 11.1, but her children, like the outer courts
of the temple in 11.2, are physically vulnerable.

Action

Satan, unable to dislodge God's people from their place of spiritual
security, turns on their vulnerable, physical dimension. He stands on
the edge of the sea (representing chaos) ready to call forth the agent of
his persecution.

REVELATION 13.1–10, 18

[13.1] And I saw a beast rising out of the sea; and on its horns were
ten diadems, and on its heads were blasphemous names. [13.2] And
the beast that I saw was like a leopard, its feet were like a bear's, and
its mouth was like a lion's mouth. And the dragon gave it his power
and his throne and great authority. [13.3] One of its heads seemed to
have received a death-blow, but its mortal wound had been healed.
In amazement the whole earth followed the beast. [13.4] They

worshiped the dragon, for he had given his authority to the beast, and they worshiped the beast, saying, 'Who is like the beast, and who can fight against it?' [13.5] The beast was given a mouth uttering haughty and blasphemous words, and it was allowed to exercise authority for forty-two months. [13.6] It opened its mouth to utter blasphemies against God, blaspheming his name and his dwelling, that is, those who dwell in heaven. [13.7] Also it was allowed to make war on the saints and to conquer them. It was given authority over every tribe and people and language and nation, [13.8] and all the inhabitants of the earth will worship it, everyone whose name has not been written from the foundation of the world in the book of life of the Lamb that was slaughtered.

[13.9] Let anyone who has an ear listen:

[13.10] If you are to be taken captive, into captivity you go; if you kill with the sword, with the sword you must be killed. Here is a call for the endurance and faith of the saints.

[13.18] This calls for wisdom: let anyone with understanding calculate the number of the beast, for it is the number of a person. Its number is six hundred and sixty-six.

Characters

In past scholarship the identity of the beast has usually been decided on the basis of the first two verses of Chapter 13. These verses portray the beast as a composite of the four beasts in Daniel 7. Daniel's beasts represented tyrannical empires, and so it has been generally assumed that John's beast must stand for a similar entity, i.e. the Roman empire (Caird 1984: 162; Mounce 1977: 251; Sweet 1990: 207; Beasley-Murray 1978: 209; Wilcock 1975: 124; Court 1994: 59; Farrer 1964: 152).

This is, however, a premature conclusion, since the body of the beast is merely a means by which the beast may be cast as a successor to its Danielic predecessors. Once this function has been fulfilled the body of the beast drops out of view and John's attention is focused solely on the head with the healed mortal wound, to the extent that this head totally represents the beast.

John changes his image of the beast, from the one described in 13.1, 2 to the beast which consists of the head with the healed mortal wound, in the course of 13.3. Here he says that, 'One of its heads seemed to have received a death-blow, but its mortal wound had been healed'.

From the Greek this verse may be rewritten: 'One of the beast's heads seemed to have received a death-blow, but the beast's mortal wound had been healed.' This is a curious thing to say in the light of the information supplied by 17.10 that the seven heads are seven Roman emperors, five of whom have fallen, one is, and one is to come. As such, these heads reign in succession, so when one falls/dies another succeeds it and the creature as a whole lives on. In order for 13.3 to be remarkable, therefore, it might be expected to read: 'One of the beast's heads seemed to have received a death-blow, but this head's mortal wound had been healed.' It does not say this because, for John, the locus of the beast's Antichristian character resides wholly in the wounded head that revives. It is therefore unnecessary for him to differentiate between the wounded head that revives and the beast, since these are one and the same.

A particular indication that John sees the whole of the beast's Antichristian character as residing in the healed wounded head may be found in 17.8, 11. In 17.8 the angel says that the beast, 'was, and is not, and is about to ascend from the bottomless pit'. In 17.11 the angel refers to the same beast saying: 'The beast that was and is not, it is an eighth but it belongs to the seven'. (The significance of 'an eighth but it belongs to the seven' is a reference to the preceding verse, where the angel reveals that: 'The seven heads...are seven kings [Roman emperors]'.) The beast is therefore, *one* of the seven emperors/heads who returns as an eighth.

That the locus of the beast's Antichristian character may not be found in the other heads of the beast is implied by 17.10, where the angel says: 'the seven heads are...seven kings, of whom five have fallen, one is living, and the other has not yet come.' This verse indicates that one of the heads 'is living', and yet, according to 17.8, 11 the beast 'is not'. The beast 'is not' in the reign of the sixth emperor because the beast 'is' only during the reigns of the fatally wounded emperor who revives as an eighth. Hence, by implication, the beast 'is not' at all times when this fatally wounded head is absent; in other words, it 'is not' during the reigns of the six emperors who do not return.

The beast, as described in Chapter 17, is, therefore, a single head that revives to become an eighth emperor. That this is the same beast that is described in Chapter 13 is indicated by two factors. First, the beast in 13.3b–18 is described as having received a mortal wound which is healed. This is parallel to the experience of the beast of 17.8, 11 which reigned, fell, and then returned to reign again. Second, the response of the dwellers on earth to the revival of both beasts is very similar, a point exemplified by a comparison of 13.8 and 17.8b. 'And all the inhabitants of the earth will worship [the beast], every one whose name has not been written from the foundation of the world in the book of life of the Lamb that was slaughtered' (13.8). 'And the inhabitants of the earth, whose names have not been written in the book of life from the foundation of the world, will be amazed when they see the beast, because it was and is not and is to come' (17.8b).

If the descriptions of the beast in Chapters 17 and 13 refer to an identical figure, and the locus of the beast's identity in Chapter 17 is the fatally wounded head that revives, then the locus of the beast's identity must be in the same head in Chapter 13. In order to establish the identity of the beast in 13.1–8, therefore, it is necessary to begin by identifying the emperor whom this head symbolizes.

The emperor to whom the fatally wounded head refers is Nero. Nero committed suicide in AD 68, but it was popularly believed that he had escaped to the east where he was mustering a Parthian force with whom he would return to recapture the Roman empire. Evidence of the potency of this legend in the popular imagination may be seen in Tacitus' accounts of the terror induced by the news of two separate impostors who claimed to be Nero returned (*Histories* 1.2 and 2.8f.). Nero's popularity amongst the Parthians, and their hope for his return, is recorded by Suetonius (*The Twelve Caesars*, 'Nero' 57). The legend survived for some time and appears in three *Sibylline Oracles* which date from between AD 79–132 (*Sibylline Oracles* 4.119–24, 137–9, 145–8; *Sibylline Oracles* 5.28–34, 93–110, 137–54, 214–27, 361–80; *Sibylline Oracles* 3.63–74). Bauckham (1993a: 407–23) provides a full account of the so-called Nero *redivivus* myth.

The final feature which secures Nero as the figure behind the beast's identity is the riddle of 13.18. The number 666 would have been interpreted by John's hearers using the ancient practice of gematria. Because numbers were represented by letters in Greek and Hebrew culture, then names could be converted into a numerical value by adding up the value of each letter in the name. The number 666 could stand for many different names, but the interpretation favoured by most scholars is Neron Caesar. Bauckham (1993a: 387) suggests that Neron Caesar is 'eminently the most preferable' solution to the puzzle, and provides a full account of the techniques and subtle complexities of gematria (1993a: 384–407).

Once Nero has been securely identified as the head which exhibits the beastly qualities of John's monster from the sea, it is possible to consider the question of where his head appears among the first seven. It has been concluded above that the beast is only active/visible when Nero (the wounded head) is reigning, and so the initial appearance of the beast must have coincided with Nero's first reign (AD 54–68). Therefore, Nero is the first of the seven heads as well as the last/eighth (cf. pp.76–7).

If it may be concluded that Nero's head is the definitive locus of the beast, and that its activity is only manifested in his reigns as first and eighth emperor, then the specific identity of the beast in 13.1–10 must be one of these two incarnations. Revelation 13.1ff. appears to describe the first emergence of the beast (parallel to 11.7), and so it is logical to suppose that the description of the beast's activities in this chapter refers to Nero's first reign. A point which causes Bauckham (1993a: 431– 50) to call this conclusion into question is the fact that the head's mortal wound is depicted as already having been healed, something which might be expected to be a feature of Nero *redivivus*, the eighth emperor. However, the reign of the beast in 13.1–8 cannot be identical with the reign of the eighth beast because these two reigns last for unmistakably different symbolic periods: the beast's reign in 13.5 is for forty-two months, while in 17.12 it is for one hour (in the company of the ten kings). The solution to this conundrum is to recognize that John uses Nero's distinctive career as a means of identifying his head to the hearers. That is to say that the healed wound is a badge of the head's identity, it is not the consequence of events which have already taken place before the beast has appeared in the story.

In summary, the locus of the beast is in the head which reigns as the first of seven emperors, is fatally wounded, but threatens to return to recapture his empire as an eighth. This head is identified as representing the emperor Nero for two reasons. First, because of the contemporary currency of the myth that Nero would return to recapture Rome. Second, because the number 666 is best interpreted as referring to Neron Caesar. The first appearance of the beast coincides with Nero's first reign, and so the first appearance of the beast in the text (13.1–10) is taken as a description of this period.

Action

The beast (Nero in his first reign) emerges from the Abyss. He takes on divine pretensions and reigns for a period of forty-two months, a traditional time-span for a period of tribulation (13.5 cf. 11.2). He makes war on the saints and conquers them (13.7 cf. 11.7).

The actions of Nero in 13.5–8 refer to his infamous persecution of Christians in Rome (Tacitus, *Annals* 15.44). This action took place following a fire, reputedly started at Nero's command, which destroyed part of the city in AD 64. At some point in the aftermath (the exact date is unclear) the Roman Christians were scapegoated by Nero and suffered appalling torture and death; tradition has it that the apostles Peter and Paul were among his victims. If John took this persecution as the point at which the beast first emerged into the open, then it is possible that the 'forty-two months' of the beast's rule stands for the literal period between Nero's persecution and his suicide in AD 68. However, it is also possible that the forty-two-month period is purely symbolic of the whole of Nero's reign.

REVELATION 13.11–18

[13.11] Then I saw another beast that rose out of the earth; it had two horns like a lamb and it spoke like a dragon. [13.12] It exercises all the authority of the first beast on its behalf, and it makes the earth and its inhabitants worship the first beast, whose mortal wound had been healed. [13.13] It performs great signs, even making fire come down from heaven to earth in the sight of all; [13.14] and by the signs that it is allowed to perform on behalf of the beast, it deceives the inhabitants of the earth, telling them to make an image for the beast that had been wounded by the sword, and yet lived, [13.15] and it was allowed to give breath to the image of the beast so that the image of the beast could even speak and cause those who would not worship the image of the beast to be killed. [13.16] Also it causes all, both small and great, both rich and poor, both free and slave, to be marked on the right hand or the forehead, [13.17] so that no one can buy or sell who does not have the mark, that is, the name of the beast or the number of its name. [13.18] This calls for wisdom: let anyone with understanding calculate the number of the beast, for it is the number of a person. Its number is six hundred and sixty-six.

Characters

Nero is assisted by the second beast (13.11–17). Although this beast is commonly identified as some form of official agent of the Roman imperial cult (e.g. Caird 1984: 171; Mounce 1977: 259; Morris 1987: 166; Bauckham 1993a: 446), there is little evidence to support this conclusion. While the emperor cult was an important aspect of civic life in first-century Asia Minor there is no evidence that the *commune Asiae*, or any other Roman authority, was responsible for enforcing emperor worship. Worship was *allowed* by the emperors of the period (Bauckham 1993a: 446), but it was never demanded by the authorities of the empire. The one known exception (in the first century) is recorded in Pliny's correspondence with Trajan (emperor AD 98–117) (Pliny, *Epistles* 10.96–7). Here Trajan affirms that those who are charged with Christianity (by a third party) should be punished if they refused to offer incense to an image of the emperor. Trajan adds that these cases should not be hunted out, which suggests that his concern was to satisfy the local accusers of the Christians rather than to enforce universal emperor worship for himself.

A consideration of the characteristics of the second beast indicates that it may represent John's opponents, the prophets Balaam and Jezebel (2.14, 20–24). The beast is commonly recognized as being local, as indicated by its rising from the land. Balaam and Jezebel were certainly that.

The beast has two horns like a lamb (13.11). That is to say that the beast looks like one of the flock of God's people who follow the Lamb. This was not true of any Roman officials, but from John's description of Balaam and Jezebel (2.14, 20) it is clear that these prophets were accepted as members of the congregations to which they belonged.

The beast speaks like a dragon (13.11). Despite the beast's Christian appearance its voice reveals its true identity as an agent of the dragon or Satan. This description corresponds to Christ's rebuke of Balaam and Jezebel for leading his followers into the eating of food sacrificed to idols (2.14, 20), immorality (2.20) and learning 'the deep things of Satan' (2.24).

The beast exercises all the authority of the first beast in its presence, and makes the earth and its inhabitants worship the first beast whose mortal wound was healed (13.12). This verse is crucial to the identity of the second beast. Given that the first beast is Nero, then it must be the case that the second beast represents a pro-Nero body. This cannot have been an official Roman figure since Nero had 'become a bogey with which to threaten Rome' (Bauckham 1993a: 416) (e.g. *Sibylline Oracles* 4.137–9, 145–8). This point is further reinforced by the following quote from Bauckham:

For much of the population of the eastern provinces of the empire, it seems (especially from Dio Chrysostom's comment) [written in Asia Minor, probably at the end of the first century, 'Even now everyone wishes he were alive, and most believe that he is' (*Orations*. 21.10)] that Nero's return was not merely the object of expectation but an object of eager hope. The philhellene emperor, friendly to the Parthians, had acquired the mythic image of a messianic saviour figure, who would wreak the vengeance of the east on the west and re-establish the rule of the east.

(Bauckham 1993a: 449–50)

Hence, far from being an official Roman body, the second beast must have been a subversive indigenous group who believed that Nero had escaped to the east and that he would return to save his allies and destroy western Rome. It is unlikely, without the power of the state behind them, that a group of this kind would normally have had much effect on John's congregations. The fact that John mentions them, and with such ferocity, suggests that they were major figures on his horizon. Balaam and Jezebel, false teachers with influence in John's churches, are the most likely candidates for this role.

The beast works great signs, even making fire come down from heaven to earth in the sight of men and by these signs it deceives those who dwell on earth into worshipping the first beast (13.13, 14). Balaam and Jezebel are both described as deceiving God's followers, and Jezebel's followers are accused of learning 'the deep things of Satan' (2.24).

The second beast is also described as giving breath to the image of the first beast and causing those who would not worship it to be slain (13.15). Three indicators suggest that this verse may be a later addition to the original text. First, there is a change of tense from the present (13.12–14), to the aorist (13.15), and back to the present (13.16–18). Abrupt changes of tense do occur in Revelation (e.g. 20.7–9), but this may usually be explained in terms of the dramatic effect created, which does not appear to be the case in this instance. Second, 13.15 contradicts 13.16, 17. In the former verse those who refuse to worship the beast (a sign of allegiance) are slain, while in the latter verses those who refuse its mark (a sign of allegiance) are merely prevented from trading. Third, there is no evidence of widespread denunciation of this type until the reign of Trajan (cf.p. 89). However, if this verse is original it is possible that it looks forward to the role of the second beast once Nero is restored to power and resumes his persecution of Christians.

The reference to the second beast's role in trade (13.17) is a further clue to its identity. Hemer (1986: 120–3) points out the importance of trade guilds, especially in Thyatira. Traders would have had to be members of a guild in order to do business, but members of a guild would also be required to attend guild feasts. The food eaten at these feasts would have been sacrificed to idols (2.20). The feasts may also have incorporated immoral practices (2.20, 22). It is also possible that these guilds looked to the returning Nero as a saviour figure. Hence, Christians were faced with a decision, either to refuse membership of the guilds and face economic hardship, or to enter them and find themselves engaged in an organization which practised immorality, the worship of idols and which may have exhibited strong support for the returning Nero. If Jezebel was encouraging Christians to join these trade guilds, as Hemer (1986: 123) suggests, then Jezebel, and those like her, displayed the character of the second beast as described in 13.17.

A final piece of evidence which points to the identification of the second beast with the prophets Balaam and Jezebel, is the common identity of the second beast of 13.11–17 and the false prophet of 16.13 and 19.20. Of the eight references to false prophets in the New Testament outside Revelation (Matthew 7.15; 24.11, 24; Mark 13.22; Luke 6.26; Acts 13.6; 2 Peter 2.1; 1 John 4.1), all but one (Acts 13.6) refer to pseudo-Christian rather than pagan figures. This suggests that it is likely that the second beast/false prophet was a figure inside the churches rather than outside them. The obvious, and only, candidates for this role are the false prophets Balaam and Jezebel. Hence, in name, appearance and actions Jezebel and Balaam fit John's description of the second beast/false prophet.

Timing

The temporal relationship between the appearance of the first and second beasts is apparently simultaneous. However, if the identification of the second beast as those who looked for the return of Nero is correct, then this beast continues to be active in the period following Nero's demise. That is, they cause people to worship him because he will return, rather than because he has returned.

Action

Jezebel, Balaam and those like them use a collection of devices in an attempt to persuade Christians that they should remain inside, or join, the local trade guilds. Those who succumb are able to trade, but at the price of compromising their allegiance to Christ through involvement in magic arts, sexual immorality and eating idol meats. The last of these activities is the antithesis of the Eucharist for, instead of declaring their fellowship with Christ and their anticipation of his return, they declare their fellowship with idols and look forward to an alternative means of salvation.

REVELATION 14.1–5

[14.1] Then I looked, and there was the Lamb, standing on Mount Zion! And with him were one hundred forty-four thousand who had his name and his father's name written on their foreheads. [14.2] And I heard a voice from heaven like the sound of many waters and like the sound of loud thunder; the voice I heard was like the sound of harpists playing on their harps, [14.3] and they sing a new song before the throne and before the four living creatures and before the elders. No one could learn that song except the one hundred forty-four thousand who have been redeemed from the earth. [14.4] It is these who have not defiled themselves with women, for they are virgins; these follow the Lamb wherever he goes. They have been redeemed from humankind as first fruits for God and the Lamb, [14.5] and in their mouth no lie was found; they are blameless.

Characters

The 144,000 with the name of Christ and his father written on their foreheads are those who have refused to worship the beast. More specifically they are the heavenly army of the Christ, comprised of those who have been faithful unto death (12.11; 13.7). The military nature of this group is indicated by their ritual cleanliness as they prepare for holy war (Caird 1984: 179; Bauckham 1993a: 210–37). Their heavenly location is made plain by their presence with the Lamb and by their being described as 'redeemed from the earth' (14.3). This is the same army that appears with Christ in 19.14.

Action

The action implied by the vision of the army of heaven is that those who have died at the hands of Nero (13.7) are caught up to heaven, following the pattern of their Lord (cf. 11.12). The fact that they are described as first fruits (14.4) implies that they are, as yet, an incomplete army (cf. 6.11).

REVELATION 15.6–16.21

[15.6] and out of the temple came the seven angels with the seven plagues, robed in pure bright linen, with golden sashes across their chests. [15.7] Then one of the four living creatures gave the seven angels seven golden bowls full of the wrath of God, who lives forever and ever; [15.8] and the temple was filled with smoke from the glory of God and from his power, and no one could enter the temple until the seven plagues of the seven angels were ended.

[16.1] Then I heard a loud voice from the temple telling the seven angels, 'Go and pour out on the earth the seven bowls of the wrath of God.'

[16.2] So the first angel went and poured his bowl on the earth, and a foul and painful sore came on those who had the mark of the beast and who worshiped its image.

[16.3] The second angel poured his bowl into the sea, and it became like the blood of a corpse, and every living thing in the sea died.

[16.4] The third angel poured his bowl into the rivers and the springs of water, and they became blood. [16.5] And I heard the angel of the waters say,

'You are just, O Holy One, who are and were, for you have judged these things; [16.6] because they shed the blood of saints and prophets, you have given them blood to drink. It is what they deserve!'

[16.7] And I heard the altar respond,

'Yes, O Lord God, the Almighty, your judgments are true and just!'

[16.8] The fourth angel poured his bowl on the sun, and it was allowed to scorch them with fire; [16.9] they were scorched by the fierce heat, but they cursed the name of God, who had authority over these plagues, and they did not repent and give him glory.

[16.10] The fifth angel poured his bowl on the throne of the beast, and its kingdom was plunged into darkness; people gnawed their tongues in agony, [16.11] and cursed the God of heaven because of their pains and sores, and they did not repent of their deeds.

[16.12] The sixth angel poured his bowl on the great river Euphrates, and its water was dried up in order to prepare the way for the kings from the east. [16.13] And I saw three foul spirits like frogs coming from the mouth of the dragon, from the mouth of the beast, and from the mouth of the false prophet. [16.14] These are demonic spirits, performing signs, who go abroad to the kings of the whole world, to assemble them for battle on the great day of God the

Almighty. [16.15] ('See, I am coming like a thief! Blessed is the one who stays awake and is clothed, not going about naked and exposed to shame.') [16.16] And they assembled them at the place that in Hebrew is called Harmagedon.

[16.17] The seventh angel poured his bowl into the air, and a loud voice came out of the temple, from the throne, saying, 'It is done!' [16.18] And there came flashes of lightning, rumblings, peals of thunder, and a violent earthquake, such as had not occurred since people were upon the earth, so violent was that earthquake.

[16.19] The great city was split into three parts, and the cities of the nations fell. God remembered great Babylon and gave her the wine-cup of the fury of his wrath. [16.20] And every island fled away, and no mountains were to be found; [16.21] and huge hailstones, each weighing about a hundred pounds, dropped from heaven on people, until they cursed God for the plague of the hail, so fearful was that plague.

Characters

Two sets of characters take part in this section of story-telling text: those who are the object of God's judgment, and the agents of that judgment. The identification of these characters requires the combination of information from Chapter 16 and the interpretative Chapter 17.

The identity of the dragon, beast and false prophet (16.13) are considered above (pp.81,84–91).

The kings of the east who cross the Euphrates (16.12) represent rulers of the Parthians who, it was widely believed, would ally themselves to Nero and return with him to conquer Rome (Bauckham 1993a: 429–30).

Location

The significance of the term Harmagedon (16.16) may not be explained in geographical terms. Harmagedon means Mount Megiddo, but no such mountain exists – there is only a city (2 Kings 23.29) and a plain (Judges 5.19–20, Zechariah 12.10–11) of that name. It is not obvious why John uses the term Harmagedon to describe this mountain, but the function and significance of this location is made plain by the relationship of this mountain to Mount Zion (14.1). Mount Zion is the place where the Lamb musters his army of martyrs for the final battle against the beast and false prophet, which they join in 19.14.

Harmagedon, by contrast, is the mountain where the dragon, beast and false prophet muster their armies for this same battle (16.13–16; cf. 17.13, 14; 19.19).

Action

The judgments which have been announced by the seal visions and trumpets are finally executed. The seven bowls of wrath are poured out on those who bore the mark of the beast, the earth, sea, rivers, sun, and the throne of the beast – the great city itself. In order to appreciate the detail of how John saw this judgment taking place it is necessary to refer to the explanation provided by Chapter 17.

REVELATION 17.1–18 – AN INTERPRETATION OF 15.6–16.21

[17.1] Then one of the seven angels who had the seven bowls came and said to me, 'Come, I will show you the judgment of the great whore who is seated on many waters, [17.2] with whom the kings of the earth have committed fornication, and with the wine of whose fornication the inhabitants of the earth have become drunk.' [17.3] So he carried me away in the spirit into a wilderness, and I saw a woman sitting on a scarlet beast that was full of blasphemous names, and it had seven heads and ten horns. [17.4] The woman was clothed in purple and scarlet, and adorned with gold and jewels and pearls, holding in her hand a golden cup full of abominations and the impurities of her fornication; [17.5] and on her forehead was written a name, a mystery: 'Babylon the great, mother of whores and of earth's abominations.' [17.6] And I saw that the woman was drunk with the blood of the saints and the blood of the witnesses to Jesus.

When I saw her, I was greatly amazed. [17.7] But the angel said to me, 'Why are you so amazed? I will tell you the mystery of the woman, and of the beast with seven heads and ten horns that carries her. [17.8] The beast that you saw was, and is not, and is about to ascend from the bottomless pit and go to destruction. And the inhabitants of the earth, whose names have not been written in the book of life from the foundation of the world, will be amazed when they see the beast, because it was and is not and is to come.

[17.9] 'This calls for a mind that has wisdom: the seven heads are seven mountains on which the woman is seated; also, they are seven kings, [17.10] of whom five have fallen, one is living, and the other has not yet come; and when he comes, he must remain only a little while. [17.11] As for the beast that was and is not, it is an eighth but it belongs to the seven, and it goes to destruction. [17.12] And the ten horns that you saw are ten kings who have not yet received a kingdom, but they are to receive authority as kings for one hour, together with the beast. [17.13] These are united in yielding their power and authority to the beast; [17.14] they will make war on the Lamb, and the Lamb will conquer them, for he is Lord of lords and King of kings, and those with him are called and chosen and faithful.'

[17.15] And he said to me, 'The waters that you saw, where the whore is seated, are peoples and multitudes and nations and languages. [17.16] And the ten horns that you saw, they and the beast will hate the whore; they will make her desolate and naked; they will devour her flesh and burn her up with fire. [17.17] For God had put it into their hearts to carry out his purpose by agreeing to give their kingdom to the beast, until the words of God will be fulfilled. [17.18] The woman you saw is the great city that rules over the kings of the earth.'

Characters

There are two sets of characters involved in the judgment scene depicted in Chapter 16 and explained in Chapter 17: the objects of judgment and the agents of judgment. This simple ordering of characters is complicated, however, by the multiple descriptions of both parties, in particular, the objects of judgment.

The objects of judgment are described in terms of their relationship to the beast, the cause of their punishment, and their geographical location. Their relationship to the beast is indicated in the first instance by their description as those who 'had the mark of the beast and who worshiped its image' (16.2). In Chapter 17 the object of judgment is alternatively described as the whore which sits on the scarlet beast that was full of blasphemous names (17.3). This beast has already been identified as Nero (cf. pp.84–7).

The second identifying mark, which is intimately connected with the first, is the action for which they are being punished – their shedding of the blood of the saints and prophets/witnesses of Jesus (16.6; 17.6).

The geographical location of the objects of judgment has two aspects: a focus and a wider area which is also affected. The focus of judgment is variously described as: 'the throne of the beast' (16.10), 'the great city' (16.19), 'Babylon' (16.19), 'the great whore who is seated on many waters' (17.1), 'Babylon the great' (17.5), the woman seated on the beast with seven heads which are seven mountains (17.8, 9), seated on many waters which are, 'peoples and multitudes and nations and languages' (17.15) and, 'the great city that rules over the kings of the earth' (17.18). On the basis of this multiple description the geographical focus of God's judgment may be identified as the city of Rome (Beckwith 1919: 690; Mounce 1977: 307; Ellul 1977: 187). Because of the vast extent of Rome's influence the wider area effected by her judgment extends to the ends of the known world: the first four bowls punish all who have received the mark of the beast (16.2–9), the kingdom of the beast is affected as well as its throne (16.10), the cities of the nations fall, as well as the great city (16.19).

The objects of judgment are therefore all those whose allegiance to Nero has implicated them in the murder of the saints, prophets and witnesses of Jesus. The principal occasion of such a slaughter would have been that of Nero's fearful persecution of Christians in Rome c. AD 65 (Tacitus, *Annals* 15.44). This event explains why Rome should be the epicentre of God's judgment. Nero's central role in this event means that not only the Romans who took part in the persecution, but also all those with an allegiance to Nero, are subject to judgment.

This identification of the object of God's judgment raises questions regarding the relationship between the whore Babylon and pseudo-prophetess Jezebel. A certain level of connection between these two appears to be indicated by their common description as female fornicators (2.20; 17.2), who have a relationship with the beast (13.11–17; 17.3), and who ultimately suffer God's judgment (2.22; 17.17). These two characters cannot be identical because Babylon is a great city, while Jezebel is a local prophet. Further, if Jezebel is the central figure behind the second beast, then she is preserved from the bowl judgments in order to appear at Harmagedon (16.13–16). However, those who follow Jezebel and Balaam and give their allegiance to Nero do become part of his consort, the whore, and so abandon their status as the bride of Christ. Thus Jezebel may be seen as having the same character as the mother of whores (and hence, so do her followers), even though her fate is reserved for a more direct confrontation with Christ.

A further group of John's hearers may be expected to be subject to the events of judgment described in 15.6–17.18, although not so directly. These are those who have placed their faith in the eternity of Rome. They will be affected by the consequences of her destruction as her wider kingdom collapses and those who are economically dependent on it suffer accordingly (18.1–19.3).

The agents of God's judgment are described in detail in Chapter 17. In 17:7–15 the angel unravels the mystery of the identity of the beast by presenting an overview of its career from start to finish (cf. pp.84–8). The angel's tour of the beast's career begins with what John has already seen: the first appearance of Nero and the reaction of the people when he disappeared (cf. 13.1ff.). That the angel refers to this first appearance is indicated by the almost direct repetition of 13.8 in 17.8. The angel then moves on to explain the period during which the beast 'is not' – the period contemporary with John's hearers (17.10). This is described as a succession of seven kings, five of whom have fallen, one of whom is currently in power and another who will reign briefly before the beast returns. Then the future reappearance of the beast is explained and described in 17.11–14. First, Nero re-emerges as an eighth emperor and the character of the beast is again displayed in full. Nero is joined in this new incarnation by the ten crowned horns (see identification below) who reign with him for 'one hour' (17.12). The angel completes the beast's life story by foreshadowing its ultimate demise at the hands of the Lamb (17.14 cf. 16.13–16 and 19.19, 20). This life story is designed to confirm the identification of the beast in terms of its unmistakable career, but this does not directly reveal which part of its career is relevant to the story of the destruction of the great city. For this information it is necessary to go on to the verses which describe the action rather than the participants. Here, in 17.16, the desolation of the whore/great city is attributed to the ten horns which act with the beast in its final hour. Hence, it may be concluded that the beast which takes part in the action of judgment at this point in the story is Nero in his second incarnation, during which he is accompanied by the ten horns.

The ten horns of the beast (17.7, 12, 16 cf. 13.1; 16.12) are described as kings in 17.12. They are the same kings who cross the Euphrates in 16.12, and may therefore be characterized as the Parthian kings who were expected to form an alliance with Nero as he re-emerged from the east (Morris 1987: 191). Their number is governed by the ten horns of Daniel's fourth beast (Daniel 7.7). Incidentally, because these horns only appear in Nero's second reign they should all be seen as issuing from the head which represents Nero in the initial image of the beast in 13.1. This provides a further, visual, emphasis to the primacy of Nero's head among the seven.

Action

The action described in 17.1–18 reviews and interprets the action of
15.6–16.21. In particular 17.1–18 provides information about the
actual mechanics of how the whore will be destroyed. The precise
means by which this judgment will be executed is described quite
plainly in 17.16 where it is stated that: 'The ten horns that you saw,
they and the beast will hate the whore; they will make her desolate and
naked; they will devour her flesh and burn her up with fire.' Thus the
means by which the consort of Nero is punished for her part in the
persecution of the saints is at the hands of her own 'lover'. This image
of the faithless woman destroyed by her faithless partner sits in direct
opposition to that of Christ's faithful bride made secure by the one who
is Faithful and True (21.2; 19.11).

This account of the action in 17.1–18 may seem unrealistically
simple in the light of the apparently complex action described in
17.7–15. However, this impression of complexity is false and may be
avoided if 17.7–15 is recognized as a description of the beast in terms of
its career, rather than a real-time account of the unfolding of that
career.

REVELATION 19.11–21.8

[19.11] Then I saw heaven opened, and there was a white horse! Its
rider is called Faithful and True, and in righteousness he judges and
makes war. [19.12] His eyes are like a flame of fire, and on his head
are many diadems; and he has a name inscribed that no one knows
but himself. [19.13] He is clothed in a robe dipped in blood, and his
name is called The Word of God. [19.14] And the armies of heaven,
wearing fine linen, white and pure, were following him on white
horses. [19.15] From his mouth comes a sharp sword with which to
strike down the nations, and he will rule them with a rod of iron; he
will tread the winepress of the fury of the wrath of God the Almighty.
[19.16] On his robe and on his thigh he has a name inscribed, 'King
of kings and Lord of lords.'
[19.17] Then I saw an angel standing in the sun, and with a loud
voice he called to the birds that fly in midheaven, 'Come, gather for
the great supper of God, [19.18] to eat the flesh of kings, the flesh of
captains, the flesh of the mighty, the flesh of horses and their riders –
flesh of all, both free and slave, both small and great.' [19.19] Then I
saw the beast and the kings of the earth with their armies gathered to

make war against the rider on the horse and against his army. [19.20] And the beast was captured, and with it the false prophet who had performed in its presence the signs by which he deceived those who had received the mark of the beast and those who worshiped its image. These two were thrown alive into the lake of fire that burns with sulfur. [19.21] And the rest were killed by the sword of the rider on the horse, the sword that came from his mouth; and all the birds were gorged with their flesh.

[20.1] Then I saw an angel coming down from heaven, holding in his hand the key to the bottomless pit and a great chain. [20.2] He seized the dragon, that ancient serpent, who is the Devil and Satan, and bound him for a thousand years, [20.3] and threw him into the pit, and locked and sealed it over him, so that he would deceive the nations no more, until the thousand years were ended. After that he must be let out for a little while.

[20.4] Then I saw thrones, and those seated on them were given authority to judge. I also saw the souls of those who had been beheaded for their testimony to Jesus and for the word of God. They had not worshiped the beast or its image and had not received its mark on their foreheads or their hands. They came to life and reigned with Christ a thousand years. [20.5] (The rest of the dead did not come to life until the thousand years were ended.) This is the first resurrection. [20.6] Blessed and holy are those who share in the first resurrection. Over these the second death has no power, but they will be priests of God and of Christ, and they will reign with him a thousand years.

[20.7] When the thousand years are ended, Satan will be released from his prison [20.8] and will come to deceive the nations at the four corners of the earth, Gog and Magog, in order to gather them for battle; they are as numerous as the sands of the sea. [20.9] They marched up over the breadth of the earth and surrounded the camp of the saints and the beloved city. And fire came down from heaven and consumed them. [20.10] And the devil who had deceived them was thrown into the lake of fire and sulfur, where the beast and the false prophet were, and they will be tormented day and night forever and ever.

[20.11] Then I saw a great white throne and the one who sat on it; the earth and the heaven fled from its presence, and no place was found for them. [20.12] And I saw the dead, great and small, standing before the throne, and books were opened. Also another book was opened, the book of life. And the dead were judged according to their works, as recorded in the books. [20.13] And the sea gave up the dead that were in it, Death and Hades gave up the dead that were in them, and all were judged according to what they had done. [20.14] Then Death and Hades were thrown into the lake of fire. This is the second death, the lake of fire; [20.15] and anyone whose name was not found written in the book of life was thrown into the lake of fire.

[21.1] Then I saw a new heaven and a new earth; for the first heaven and the first earth had passed away, and the sea was no more. [21.2] And I saw the holy city, the new Jerusalem, coming down out of heaven from God, prepared as a bride adorned for her husband. [21.3] And I heard a loud voice from the throne saying, 'See, the home of God is among mortals. He will dwell with them as their God; they will be his peoples, and God himself will be with them; [21.4] he will wipe every tear from their eyes. Death will be no more; mourning and crying and pain will be no more; for the first things have passed away.'

[21.5] And the one who was seated on the throne said, 'See, I am making all things new.' Also he said, 'Write this, for these words are trustworthy and true.' [21.6] Then he said to me, 'It is done! I am the Alpha and the Omega, the beginning and the end. To the thirsty I will give water as a gift from the spring of the water of life. [21.7] Those who conquer will inherit these things, and I will be their God and they will be my children. [21.8] But as for the cowardly, the faithless, the polluted, the murderers, the fornicators, the sorcerers, the idolaters, and all liars, their place will be in the lake that burns with fire and sulfur, which is the second death.'

Characters

The only new characters in this portion of story-telling text are Gog and Magog. The image of Gog and Magog in prophecy concerned with the End appears to have its origin in Ezekiel 38.2. These figures, or those like them, are developed as apocalyptic enemies in later literature (Beckwith 1919: 744; Sweet 1990: 291; Mounce 1977: 362). As such they symbolize the ancient enemies of God's people who must be defeated before the End. By bringing Gog and Magog onto the scene John embraces ancient prophetic expectation with regard to the Final conflict.

The rider on the white horse has not previously been depicted in these terms, but the multiple descriptions of 19.11–16 compound his identification as Jesus Christ, the warrior Messiah (cf. 5.6f. and 14.1f.).

Action

This section of story-telling text portrays the much anticipated battle between the beast with his allies and the Lamb with his allies (cf. 16.13–16; 17.14). Once Nero and his Parthian allies have destroyed imperial Rome and have set themselves up as rulers in place of the preceding emperor, they reign for just 'one hour' before the final conflict deposes them (cf. 17.12). The messianic warrior and his armies (cf. 14.1–5) sweep down from heaven to do battle with the beast (Nero), the false prophets (Jezebel and Balaam), and the kings of the earth who have formed alliance with Nero (19.11–21). The Messiah captures and disposes of Nero, his propagandists, and his lesser associates (19.20, 21).

As a result Satan is again exposed. This time, instead of being hurled from heaven to earth, he is taken to a still lower level of the universe and is sealed in the Abyss for a thousand years (20.1–3).

With Nero and Satan removed from the earth the Messiah is able to establish his rule there, with the martyrs, for as long as Satan is in the Abyss (20.4–7).

After the thousand years Satan makes a final assault on the saints with an army of all the remaining enemies of God's people (20.7–9b). That this army is comprised of every remaining enemy is indicated by the use of three images. 'From the four corners of the earth' suggests a totality of space (Mounce 1977: 362). The reference to 'Gog and Magog', the ancient enemies of Israel, suggests a totality of time. 'They are as numerous as the sands of the sea' suggests a totality of number. These enemies are consumed by fire from heaven. This may mean that they are sent directly to the lake of fire, or it may mean that they are sent to the Abyss prior to final judgment. Meanwhile, Satan is thrown into the lake of fire (20.9b–10).

With all the contestants to his rule defeated, God judges the remainder of those who have not yet been judged (20.11–15). Those whose names were not found in the book of life are thrown into the lake of fire, which presumably means that those in the book are resurrected. Hades (which contains Death), is then also thrown into the lake of fire (20.14).

With evil expelled from heaven and earth, and the destruction of death and chaos, God's perfect rule amongst his people begins (21.1–8).

THE STORY SUMMARIZED IN DIAGRAMS

The following diagrammatic summary is designed to show the broad flow of the events depicted in 12.1–14.5; 15.6–16.21; 19.11b–21.8.

AN INTRODUCTION TO THE DIAGRAMS

The universe

The identification of a three-tier universe is based on its initial description in 5.3: 'No one in heaven or on earth or under the earth was able to open the scroll or to look into it.' This statement is an emphatic pronouncement with regard to the absence of anyone, anywhere, to open the scroll. It may therefore be deduced that no other area of the universe exists. A certain amount of confusion is created by the multiple designations of the nether world: Abyss, Hades, Death, sea, under the earth. However, it is possible to demonstrate that these all represent different expressions of the same shadowy location. For example, the interchangeability of the Abyss and the sea is noted by A.Y. Collins (1976: 165–6,170–1). Also, the reference to Christ as having the keys to Death and Hades (1.18) may have a parallel in the angel of 20.1 having the key of the Abyss. Finally, if the sea/Abyss and Death and Hades are part of the same dimension of the universe, then this would explain why there is no longer any sea in 21.1 after the destruction of Death and Hades in 20.14 (two verses earlier).

The lake of fire is an exception. This is clearly separate from Hades/Abyss, since characters are taken from Hades/Abyss and thrown into the lake of fire (20.10, 15); indeed Hades itself is thrown there (20.14). That this is not included in 5.3 may indicate that nothing may be resurrected after being thrown there. The only information which the text gives with regard to the location of the lake of fire is that it is 'other' than the inhabitable universe, hence its position outside the habitable universe in the diagram below. The lake of fire is not mentioned in the story-telling text until 19.20, and for this reason does not appear in the sequence of diagrams until this point.

The cast

This three-part universe is inhabited by a concentric cast of characters, where each character has a counterpart on the opposing side. The only major character with no counterpart is God the Creator. This

enthroned figure is seen as presiding as sovereign over the battle between good and evil. The forces of good and evil are led by Christ and Satan. The cohorts of these two leaders are comprised of various angelic and human figures, including the members of the churches to whom the revelation is addressed. These opposing allegiances are denoted thus:

Allied to Christ   Allied to Satan

Specific figures which take part in the action at a particular point will be noted within these blocks of shading. When the location of a character is not specifically noted it may be assumed on the basis of previous diagrams.

Movement

Movement within the universe is denoted by a light arrow. Attack launched by one party on another is denoted by a heavy arrow.

THE STORY IN DIAGRAMS

12.1–6   The messianic community gives birth to Christ. Satan attacks Christ, who, in martyrdom, is caught up to heaven. (This scene may be seen as depicting heavenly events (Beckwith 1919: 617), but the result is the same – Christ defeats Satan through martyrdom.)

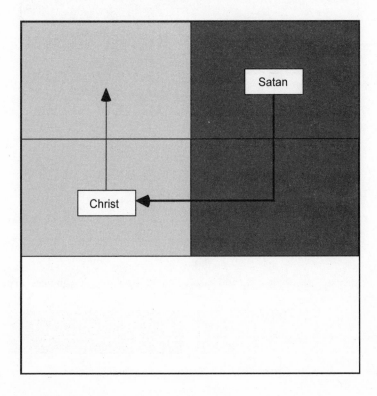

12.7–9 (10–12)   Christ's victory enables the armies of heaven to cast out Satan and his armies.

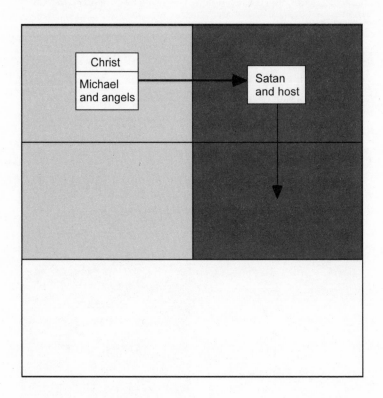

Once Satan and his host have been cast down from heaven Christ's reign in heaven is complete and unchallenged.

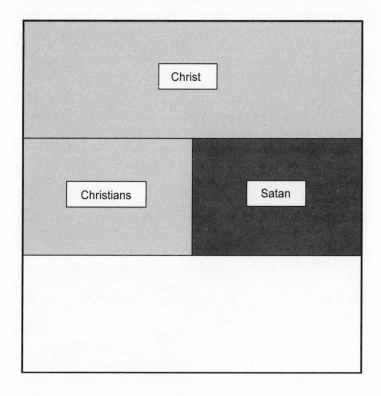

12.13–13.10   Now on earth Satan's enmity becomes focused on the messianic community (12.13). When she escapes to spiritual safety (12.16) Satan's attention turns to the destruction of Christians (12.17). His attack is carried out by the agency of Nero (the beast from the sea). Nero is enabled to defeat the saints through his persecution of them in Rome in AD 65 (13.7), but they, following the pattern of Christ, are caught up to heaven where they become part of Christ's heavenly army (**14.1–5**, cf. 7.1–17; 11.12). It is this event which makes Nero and Rome subject to God's judgment, along with all those who are associated with them.

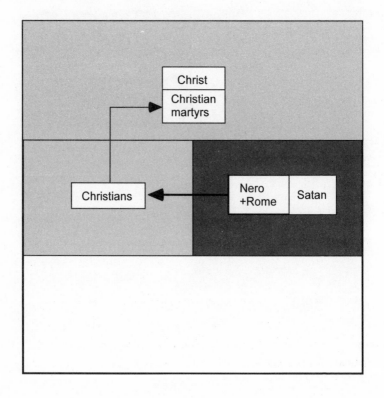

13.11–18   After Nero's fall he is succeeded by six emperors who do not expressly manifest the persecuting character of the beast. However, Rome is still due for punishment because of her part in the persecution of Christians under Nero. Meanwhile Jezebel and those like her (the second beast/false prophet) continue the cult of Nero. Economic pressure is brought to bear on John's hearers in order to persuade them to join the followers of Nero.

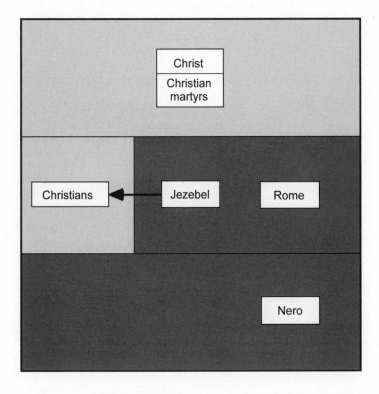

15.6–16.21 Judgment is executed on Rome and on all those who are implicated in the events of Nero's persecution of Christians. This is achieved, under God, by means of Nero himself and his allies the Parthians. They emerge from the nether regions of the Abyss/from across the Euphrates.

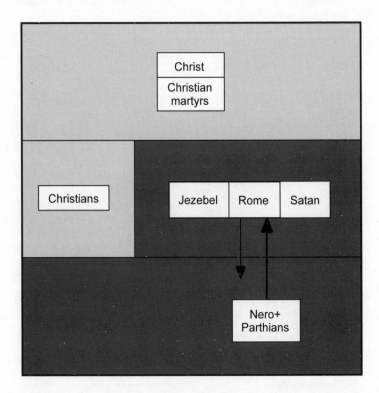

With Nero restored to power the dragon, beast and false prophet form
an unholy trinity on earth (16.13). It is not explicitly stated in the text,
but Nero's return may be expected to be accompanied by a resumption
of the beast's persecution.

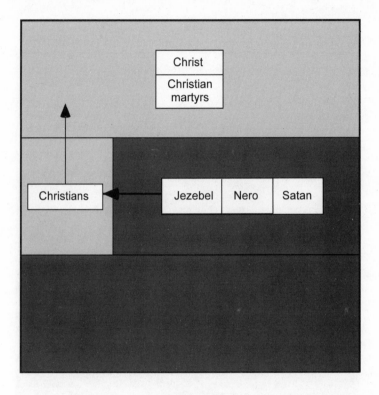

19.11b–20.3   The messianic rider and his armies (cf. 14.1–5) sweep down from heaven to do battle with Nero *redivivus*, Jezebel/Balaam and Satan himself. Christ captures Nero and the false prophets, as well as their lesser associates, and disposes of them in the lake of fire (19.20, 21). With his agents deposed Satan is again exposed, but is sealed in the Abyss for a thousand years (20.1–3).

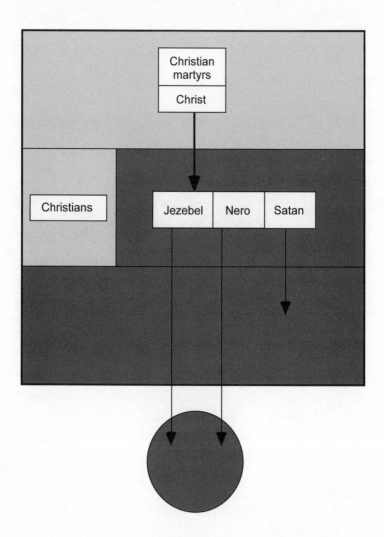

With Nero and Satan removed from the earth the Messiah is able to establish his rule there, with the Martyrs, for as long as Satan is in the Abyss (20.4–7).

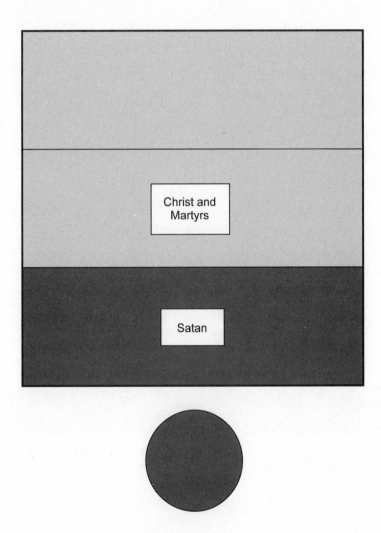

20.7–9b After the thousand years Satan makes a final assault on the saints with an army comprising all the remaining enemies of God's people.

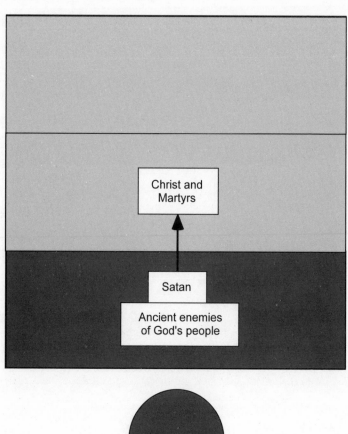

20.9b–10   The ancient enemies of God's people are consumed by fire from heaven. (It is unclear whether this event means that they are sent directly to the lake of fire, or killed – sent to the Abyss – judged – sent to lake of fire.) Satan is then finally thrown into the lake of fire.

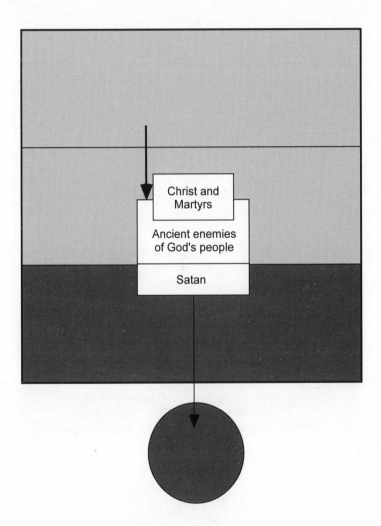

20.11–15   With all the contestants of his rule defeated God judges the remainder of those who have not yet been judged. Those whose names are not found in the book of life are thrown into the lake of fire, which implies that those whose names are found in the book of life are resurrected. Then Hades (which contains Death) is also thrown into the lake of fire.

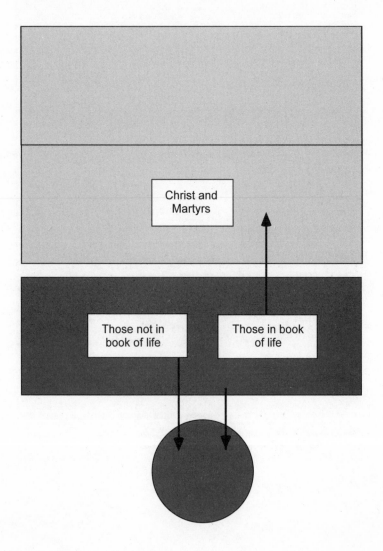

21.1–8 With evil expelled from heaven and earth, and the destruction of Death and chaos, God's perfect rule amongst his faithful people begins.

God
Christ
Christians

Chapter 6

Why this story?

The interpretation of the story of 'what must soon take place', described in Chapter 5, provides a specific account of how John saw his hearers' immediate future. In this vision John depicted Nero as the destroyer of Rome who would return after Domitian had reigned for a 'little while' (17.10). In reality, however, Nero did not return and Rome did not fall for several generations. So, was John simply mistaken, or is there some other explanation for his depiction of this particular future?

To answer this question it is necessary to start with a recognition that the overall purpose of Revelation was not simply to impart information about the future, but to inspire an active response from its hearers. The nature of this response is indicated in the seven messages. Here the churches are called to repent of attitudes and actions which are not in keeping with an exclusive allegiance to Christ (e.g. 2.5, 16, 20–23; 3.3, 19). Conversely, they are commended for those occasions when they have held fast to this allegiance, despite the cost (e.g. 2.3, 10, 13, 19, 24, 25; 3.4, 8, 10, 11). The commission to conquer, with which each of the seven messages closes, crystallizes the response for which the text calls: to remain faithful to Christ even to the point of death, and in this way to conquer 'just as I have conquered' (3.21 cf. 12.11).

However, this call for an exclusive allegiance to Christ was not made in a vacuum, rather there were a number of competing calls for allegiance in the environment of John's hearers. These competing calls offered their own visions of the future as an important element of their appeal (much as politicians today promise a brighter future under their government in order to win our votes). Hence, in order to combat these competing calls for allegiance John's text had to overturn his opponents' visions of the future.

JOHN'S STORY AS POLEMIC RESPONSE

Supporters of Rome

Those who believed in Rome's impregnable power would have seen the future as a continuation of the status quo. In this future the prosperity and peace brought by Roman rule could be expected to continue for all those who were willing to co-operate with her.

Rome's ability to survive the most appalling disasters (e.g. the year of the four emperors, AD 68–9), and the lack of any serious competition to her military might, meant that there was ample evidence to support the view that Rome would continue to be supreme in the future. It is therefore likely that this view would have been influential in John's churches. This appears to have been especially the case in Laodicea, where the Christians' self-satisfaction (3.17) indicates that they were not anxious for any change in the present order (see also 18.4).

According to John's view of the future, however, Rome's future was one in which, rather than lasting to eternity, she is doomed to destruction. John's vision of the specific cause of Rome's downfall made use of the popular belief that Nero would return to recapture the empire. However, John reworked this myth so as to cast Nero *redivivus* as the demonic servant of Satan (13.1), who is indirectly the agent of God's judgment (17.17). Rome's final destruction, as foreshadowed by the seal and trumpet visions, is eventually consummated in the bowl visions of 15.6–16.21. The interpretation of these visions (17.1–18) confirms John's prediction that mighty Rome is to be destroyed, contrary to the specific expectation of Rome's supporters (cf. pp.96–9).

Supporters of Nero

A view of the future which had a strong currency in Asia Minor *c.* AD 80 was the belief that Nero would return from the east to recapture the Roman empire (Tacitus, *Histories* 1.2 and 2.8f.; Suetonius, *The Twelve Caesars*, 'Nero' 57; *Sibylline Oracles* 4. 119–24,. 137–9, 145–8; *Sibylline Oracles* 5. 28–34, 93–110, 137–54, 214–27, 361–80; *Sibylline Oracles* 3. 63–74; cf. Bauckham 1993a: 407–23 for a full account of the so-called Nero *redivivus* myth.)

For the eastern peoples of the empire the prospect of Nero's return was a potential source of hope. For some Nero took on the quality of a messianic saviour figure, who would wreak the vengeance of the east on the west (cf. pp. 84–90). The presence of this hope in John's churches is argued on pp.88–91, where Jezebel and Balaam are identified as Nero's propagandists – the second beast. These two false prophets clearly had influence in Pergamum and Thyatira and so this is a future hope with which John was bound to engage.

John's response to the Nero myth was not to reject it entirely, but to enlarge upon it for his own purposes. He used the popular image of the returning Nero as a credible image of the threat to Rome's permanent stability, but looked further into the future to predict that Nero's second reign would last only 'one hour' (17.12). Even during this short reign Nero and his allies are shown as earmarked for destruction by the Lamb (17.14). This destruction is then foreseen as taking place at the battle of Harmagedon when Nero and his allies are all thrown into the lake of fire, from which there is no possibility of resurrection (19.19–21). Hence, John's vision of the future was shaped by the future expectations of his hearers, going beyond these expectations to overturn them.

Traditional Judaism

The traditional Jewish view of the future was one which looked forward to the fulfilment of God's promises to those who faithfully kept the Law. These promises included membership of a glorious messianic kingdom whose capital would be Jerusalem and whose king would be a new David (e.g. 1 Kings 9.5; Psalm 2.8; Isaiah 45.14; 52.7–9; 54.1–17; Daniel 2.44; 7.9–27: *Sibylline Oracles* 3.767–95; 1 *Enoch* 90.16–38; *Psalms of Solomon* 17.41, 46; 18.6–10; *Jubilees* 23.27–31). (See Shürer 1979: 497–509, for a tracing of the development of Jewish eschatology; also, Rowland 1985: 87–92.) A notable element of this future hope, contemporary with John's text, was the expectation that this messianic kingdom would last for a limited period. A clear example of this may be found in 4 *Ezra* 7.28 (*c.* AD 100, according to Charlesworth 1983: 520), according to which the faithful Jews would be resurrected into an earthly messianic kingdom which would last for a period of four hundred years.

Evidence of pressure on John's Christians to adopt a traditional Jewish view of the future may be found in the messages to the churches at Smyrna and Philadelphia. John's reference to 'the slander of those who say that they are Jews and are not' (2.9; 3.9) suggests that traditional Jews were accusing John's Christians of not being true Jews. This was a serious accusation in an environment where the right to be called

'Jew' denoted a person's status as a member of God's chosen people, the inheritors of his future promises.

Support for the theory that local Jews were claiming that John's Christians were outside God's covenant people may be found in the message to the Philadelphians. In this message Christ describes himself as the one who, 'has the key of David, who opens and no one will shut, who shuts and no one opens'. This phrase echoes Isaiah 22.22 in which a steward is given the keys of access to the king (Caird 1984: 51). Christ therefore presents himself as the one who determines who may enter God's presence, and then goes on to assure the Philadelphians that he has set before them an open door (to God's kingdom) which no one is able to shut (3.8). This promise would have formed a suitable response to Jewish suggestions that the Christians were debarred from God's heavenly kingdom by virtue of their divorce from traditional Judaism. In the following verse Christ assures the Philadelphians that not only are they loved by God, but that the Jews will be made to see that this is the case. This implies that the traditional Jews had been claiming that the Christians were deserted by God. The closing promise of this message (3.12) also has the character of a response to Jewish accusations. Here Christ assures the Philadelphians of a permanent place in God's temple in the new Jerusalem; a place to which the traditional Jews would have made an exclusive claim.

The influence of the traditional Jewish view of the future on the shape of John's story may be detected most particularly in 20.3–21.8 where John predicts the millennial reign of Christ and the realization of the new Jerusalem. In these two elements of the story John incorporates, expands and adapts Jewish expectation. Hence, a period of limited messianic reign is included, but those who are resurrected to enjoy it are those who have been faithful to Christ, rather than to the Law. Subsequently, in the imagery of the new Jerusalem, John's vision wipes away the prospect of a narrow, local new Jerusalem which was the expected reward of the traditional Jews. Instead a colossal new Jerusalem comes down from heaven which encompasses all people of all races whose faithfulness to Christ entitles them to membership of this holy city (cf. 7.9–17).

Summary

This section has begun to explore the relationship between the views of the future espoused by John's opponents and the content of John's story. Despite the limited nature of this survey there is evidence to suggest that the shape of John's story was designed as a polemic response to his opponents' future expectations and the calls for allegiance with which they were associated.

THE BASIS OF JOHN'S RESPONSE

The situation of John's hearers may account for the content of John's story, but this does not explain the basis on which these predictions were made. Did John simply make up his prognostications, or did he have a more authoritative basis for his vision of the future?

To answer this question it is necessary to recognize that predictions of the future are profoundly influenced by perceptions of the present. Hence, observers of a battlefield on which armies A and B are preparing for combat may predict a victory for army A on the basis of a present perception of its superior strength.

This connection between present perception and future prediction was crucial to the forecasts of John's opponents. For example: the supporters of Rome predicted Rome's future supremacy on the grounds of her existing and unchallenged power, the Neroans saw themselves as an ascendant force because of their belief that Nero was currently alive and gathering strength in the east, and the traditional Jews saw themselves as victorious in the future on the basis of their existing understanding of themselves as God's chosen people.

The relationship between present perception and future prediction means that a change in the former is likely to effect a change in the latter. Hence, the predicted outcome of the battle between armies A and B may be reversed if the observers' field of vision is enlarged to include massive reinforcements for army B which had previously been out of sight. This invites the possibility that John's challenge to his opponents' views of the future was based on an alternative view of the present, from which his alternative view of the future necessarily flowed.

John's view of the present represents an enlargement on, as well as an alteration of, that of his opponents. As he is taken up to heaven (4.1–5.14) he sees the universe and the organization of power within it from an entirely new perspective. From his new vantage point he sees God as sovereign over the whole universe, with Christ as the eternal victor over evil by means of his faithful death and resurrection.

John's vision of the present specifically contradicted that of Rome's supporters by presenting Christ as the victorious agent of the universal emperor, whose court supremely surpassed the grandeur of Rome (4.2–

5.14) (cf. Aune 1983). From John's heavenly vantage point it was possible for him to reveal that, while Rome appeared almighty for the dwellers on earth, it was as nothing compared to the might and sovereignty of the creator and ruler of the universe.

John's vision of the present specifically contradicted that of Jezebel and those who looked for salvation from Nero by presenting God and Christ as the One who was, is and is to come (4.8), unlike their 'saviour', who was, is not and is to come before going to destruction (17.8, 11) (Bauckham 1993a: 384).

John's vision of the present specifically contradicted that of the Jews by presenting Christ as the divinely appointed Lion of Judah, the root of David (5.5). This assertion of Christ's claim to be the eternal Davidic king was an act of definition of the true Israel: those who were allied to Israel's king were true Jews, while those who denied him were not. In 7.1–8, John portrays those who are to be spiritually protected by the seal of God's ownership as both 'the servants of our God' (7.3) and 'out of every tribe of the people of Israel' (7.4), thus confirming that the faithful hearers were encouraged to see themselves as the true Israel in the present.

It was therefore John's vision of the present, in which Christ is eternally victorious over evil, that provided the basis for his prediction that all those who were opposed to Christ and allied to Satan must ultimately be defeated. In the light of this understanding of Christ's eternal victory John was able to predict that his opponents' views of the future would prove to be incomplete.

Conclusion

Revelation begins with a promise to reveal the story of 'what must soon take place' (1.1) and then goes on to confuse us utterly. The order of story events makes no sense, giving the appearance of having been chopped up and reassembled in an almost random order. Various scholarly efforts to account for this confusion have been undertaken without success. As Fiorenza (1985: 46) says, 'Attempts to explain the sequence of visions or the total composition of Revelation either by a linear or cyclic understanding of time have not succeeded in presenting a convincing interpretation'.

This reading claims to solve the age-old problem. Bauckham (1993a: 263) recognized that the story of 'what must soon take place' is contained within the scroll which is opened by the Lamb. In order to find the story, therefore, it is necessary to find those parts of the text which reveal the contents of this scroll. Markers within the text indicate that different parts of the text have different functions. For example: some have the function of foreshadowing the contents of the scroll so as to create suspense, others have the function of reviewing and interpreting these contents, and some have the function of opening and closing the six separate instalments in which the text was designed to be heard. With the benefit of this understanding of the different internal functions performed by each section it has been possible to disclose a new structural understanding of Revelation. This structure reveals how the whole text contributes to the presentation of a convincing and engaging account of 'what must soon take place'.

At the centre of the text's structural organization are the three passages which directly divulge the contents of the Lamb's scroll (12.1–14.5; 15.6–16.21; 19.11b–21.8). When the symbolic characters and actions within these passages are interpreted they reveal a coherent and specific account of 'what must soon take place'. This story (starting from *c.* AD 80) may be summarized as follows: a short reign for Domitian after Titus, the destruction of Rome at the hands of a revived Nero with his Parthian allies, the destruction of Nero and his allies (including Jezebel) by the returning Christ, the establishment of Christ's millennial kingdom, the final onslaught of Satan from the Abyss, the destruction of Satan, the Final judgment, and the realization of the new heaven and new earth in which God dwells in perfect communion with his faithful people.

It is a cliché of mountaineering that many false peaks are climbed before the summit is achieved. The identification of the structure of Revelation and the interpretation of the story of 'what must soon take place' give access to new peaks, but from this elevation a new range of questions are brought into view. At least one of these, provoked by the apparent non-fulfilment of John's predictions, is: 'Why did John tell this particular story?'

In Chapter 6 it was concluded that John's future prediction was made in response to the future prognostications of his opponents. The effect of these competing views of the future was to influence the allegiances of John's hearers, inviting them to follow the traditional Jews, Rome or the supporters of Nero, in the interests of a brighter future. John's means of overturning his opponents' arguments was not so much by providing an alternative view of the future but by revealing an enlarged and authoritative vision of the eternal present. This present is dominated by the sovereign God, and by the Lamb who is eternally victorious over evil by means of his faithful death and resurrection. In the light of this present, no future that excludes the ultimate victory of Christ, and of the way of Christ, can stand.

Readers of Revelation in the present day have perceptions of the future that differ from those of John's opponents. However, John's view of the universe may still be used to set our current perceptions of the present and future in their wider spiritual context. When we allow our perceptions of the present to be transformed in this way, then it is no longer possible to imagine that western capitalism will survive to eternity, or that its unjust dealings with poorer nations will go unpunished. When we see our world through John's eyes, then violent revolution, while possibly an instrument of God's judgment, is shown to be a false hope for ultimate liberation. John's vision also reminds Christians of their heritage as God's covenant people, who enjoy his protection and the prospect of the consummation of that communion which is now experienced only in part. Finally, when our present is seen in its wider context, then the reader is reminded that only Christ is the victor and only the way of Christ brings victory over evil. This most important aspect of John's revelation invites a response not only of intellectual assent, but of exclusive allegiance to Christ and faithful action in the way of Christ.

Appendix: Roman emperors

Augustus   31 BC–AD 14
  (became emperor in 27 BC)

Tiberius   AD 14–37

Gaius (Caligula)   37–41

Claudius   41–54

Nero   54–68

Galba   68–69

Otho   69–69

Vitellius   69–69

Vespasian   69–79

Titus   79–81

Domitian   81–96

Nerva   96–98

Trajan   98–117

Hadrian   117–138

Select bibliography

Aune, D.E. (1983) 'The influence of the Roman imperial court ceremonial on Revelation of John', *Biblical Research* 28: 5–26.

—— (1986) 'The Apocalypse of John and the problem of genre', *Semeia* 36: 65–96.

Austin, J.L. (1955) *How to do things with words*, Cambridge, MA: Harvard University, William James Lectures.

Barr, D.L. (1986) 'The Apocalypse of John as oral enactment', *Interpretation* 40: 243–56.

Bauckham, R. (1993a) *The Climax of Prophecy*, Edinburgh: T. & T. Clark.

—— (1993b) *The Theology of the Book of Revelation*, Cambridge: Cambridge University Press.

Beale, G.K. (1984) *The Use of Daniel in Jewish Apocalyptic Literature and in the Revelation of St John*, Lanham, MD: University Press of America.

Beasley-Murray, G.R. (1978) *The Book of Revelation*, London: Oliphants.

Beckwith, I.T. (1919) *The Apocalypse of John*, Grand Rapids, MI: Baker.

Bell, A.A. Jr (1979) 'The date of John's Apocalypse. The evidence of some Roman historians reconsidered', *NTS* 25: 97–9.

Boismard, M-E. (1949) ' "L'Apocalypse", ou "Les Apocalypses" de s. Jean', *Revue biblique* 56: 507–641.

Brown, G. and Yule, G. (1983) *Discourse Analysis*, Cambridge: Cambridge University Press.

Caird, G.B. (1984) *The Revelation of St John the Divine*, 2nd edn, London: A. & C. Black.

Charles, R.H. (1920) *Revelation*, Edinburgh: T. & T. Clark.

Charlesworth, J. H. (1983) *The Old Testament Pseudepigrapha*, vol. 1, London: Darton, Longman & Todd.

Chatham, S. (1978) *Story and Discourse: Narrative Structure in Fiction and Film*, London: Cornell.

Coburn, A. (1992) *The Masters of Luxor* (the 'Doctor Who' scripts), London: Titan.

Collins, A.Y. (1984) *Crisis and Catharsis*, Philadelphia: Westminster Press.

—— (1976) *The Combat Myth in the Book of Revelation*, Missoula, MT: Scholars Press.

Collins, J.J. (1979) 'Towards the morphology of a genre', *Semeia* 14: 1–20.

Cotterell, P. and Turner, M. (1989) *Linguistics and Biblical Interpretation*, London: SPCK.

Court, J.M. (1979) *Myth and History in the Book of Revelation*, London: SPCK.
——(1994) *Revelation*, Sheffield: JSOT Press.
Cullmann, O. (1953) *Early Christian Worship*, London: SCM.
Dickens, C. (1986) *The Pickwick Papers* (first published 1837), Oxford: Oxford University Press.
Ellul, J. (1977) *Apocalypse*, New York: Seabury Press.
Esler, P.F. (1994) *The First Christians in Their Social Worlds*, London: Routledge.
Farrer, A.M. (1964) *The Revelation of Saint John the Divine*, London: SCM.
Fiorenza, E.S. (1985) *The Book of Revelation: Justice and Judgment*, Philadelphia: Fortress Press.
——(1991) *Revelation: Vision of a Just World*, Edinburgh: T. & T. Clark.
Ford, J.M. (1975) *Revelation*, New York: Doubleday.
Frend, W.H.C. (1965) *Martyrdom and Persecution in the Early Church*, Oxford: Blackwell.
Gaechter, P. (1948) 'The role of memory in the making of Revelation', *Theological Studies* 9: 419–52.
Garrow, A.J.P. (1994) 'What is and What is to Come: The serialized story in the book of Revelation', M Phil, Coventry University.
Giblin, C.H. (1991) *The Book of Revelation: The Open Book of Prophecy*, Collegeville, MN: Liturgical Press.
Hamer, M. (1987) *Trollope's Serial Fiction*, Cambridge: Cambridge University Press.
Hellholm, D. (1986) 'The problem of apocalyptic genre', *Semeia* 36: 13–64.
——(1983) (ed.) *Apocalypticism in the Mediterranean World and the Near East*, Tübingen: J.C.B. Mohr.
Hemer, C.J. (1986) *The Letters to the Seven Churches of Asia in Their Local Setting*, Sheffield: JSOT Press.
Kiddle, M. (1940) *The Revelation of St John*, London: Hodder & Stoughton.
Kreuziger, F.A. (1982) *Apocalyptic and Science Fiction*, Chicago: Scholars Press.
Ladd, G.E. (1972) *A Commentary on the Revelation of John*, Grand Rapids, MI: Eerdman.
Lambrecht, J. (1980) (ed.) *L'Apocalypse Johannique et L'Apocalyptique dans le Nouveau Testament*, Gembloux: Duculot.
Lauritzen, M. (1981) *Jane Austen's Emma on television: a study of a BBC classic serial*, Göteborg: Acta Univ Gothoburgensis.
Lodge, D. (1992) *The Art of Fiction*, London: Penguin.
Longacre, R.E. (1983) *The Grammar of Discourse*, London and New York: Plenum.
Magie, D. (1950) *Roman Rule in Asia Minor*, Princeton, NJ: Princeton University Press.
Mazzaferri, F.D. (1989) *The Genre of the Book of Revelation: from a Source Critical Perspective*, Berlin and New York: de Gruyter.
Morris, L. (1987) *Revelation*, 2nd edn, Leicester: IVP.
Mounce, R.H. (1977) *The Book of Revelation*, Grand Rapids, MI: Eerdman.
Olsson, B. (1985) 'A decade of text-linguistic analysis of Biblical texts at Uppsala', *Studia Theologica* 39: 107–26.
Palmer, D.G. (1988) *Sliced Bread: The Four Gospels and Revelation – Their Literary Structures*, Cardiff: Ceridwen Press.

Price, S.R.F. (1984) *Rituals and Power: The Roman Imperial Cult in Asia Minor*, Cambridge: Cambridge University Press.

Rhoads, D. and Michie, D. (1982) *Mark as Story*, Philadelphia: Fortress Press.

Robinson, J.A.T. (1976) *Redating the New Testament*, London: SCM.

Rowland, C. (1985) *Christian Origins*, London: SPCK.

——(1993) *Revelation*, London: Epworth.

Shürer, E. (1979) *The History of the Jewish People in the Age of Jesus Christ*, Edinburgh: T. & T. Clark.

Sperber, D. and Wilson, D. (1986) *Relevance: Communication and Cognition*, Oxford: Blackwell.

Sweet, J. (1990) *Revelation*, 2nd edn, London: SCM and ITP.

Swete, H.B. (1907) *The Apocalypse of St John*, London: Macmillan.

Thompson, L.L. (1990) *The Book of Revelation: Apocalypse and Empire*, Oxford: Oxford University Press.

Traugott, E.C. and Pratt, M.L. (1980) *Linguistics for Students of Literature*, New York: Harcourt Brace Jovanovich.

Wilcock, M. (1975) *The Message of Revelation*, Leicester: IVP.

Index of subjects

Index of references to biblical and other ancient literature

3 Apocrypha and Pseudepigrapha

4 Further ancient literature